ANGE
The Life of a Street Kid

Rebecca Dorothy Valastro

UPL Books

UPL Books
Sydney, NSW 2001
www.uplproductions.com

Publisher's Note: This is a work of fiction. Names, characters, places, and incidents are a product of the author's imagination. Locales and public names are sometimes used for atmospheric purposes. Any resemblance to actual people, living or dead, or to businesses, companies, events, institutions, or locales is completely coincidental.

ANGE The Life of a Street Kid
Rebecca Dorothy Valastro
ISBN 978-0-9954253-9-2

DEDICATION

For UPL

The Beginning

ACKNOWLEDGMENTS

Words cannot express the amount of gratitude I feel for my family. You were there for me, allowing me the time to heal. Without your continual support, Ange's story would remain untold. There are not enough words to express how much I love you.

Dr. Jerry Schwartz, you truly are a unique human being; a guardian angel. Thank you for your belief in me and in UPL Productions. It is because of your support Ange's story will reach cinema screens in the movie 7DAYS.

To my beautiful friends, each of you has brought something to this book. Your words, your stories, your care of me, have continued to inspire me, to make me strive for more. I love you all and I am grateful for each and every one of you.

Caroline DeVuono, you very special woman. Thank you so very much for helping me to refocus on this journey and thank you for inspiring the cover.

Veda Todd you amazing artist and friend, thank you for your help and expertise. I love you. And equally Chris Tasic, your help is greatly appreciated.

And to All the children in the world who battle on our streets every day and every night, this monstrosity and the abuse that led you there must stop.

CHAPTER ONE

ESCAPE

Falling to my knees, I tried to catch my breath. My heart felt as though it was trying to push its way to the outside of my chest. I wiped away the hair that had fallen across my face and felt cold liquid running down my arm. It was too dark to see but I knew it was my blood. I could feel the throb from the side of my head. I heard nothing at all in my right ear, not the sound of the wind, not the dogs barking in the distance, not even the pant from my own breath. I looked around trying to work out where I was, which direction I needed to go in, but I saw nothingness.

'I'm scared God,' I called out into the dark. Whoever you are, do you even exist? All that replied was a voice from inside, screaming at me to get up. You can't stop now! Get up!

I managed to get myself back up onto my feet and continued to run through the field. The grass was long and cut into my knees. More cold liquid ran down my legs. I didn't know how many fields I had passed through; three, four, maybe five? I was confused. I knew my way there to the willow when the sun was out to guide me (I made sure of that) but now it was dark, with no moon to light the way and my eyes were ballooning by the second. Six hours till daylight and I knew that I couldn't get lost, not now and there was no way I could turn back. If I could just reach the willow, she would be there. She would help me. She would tell me what next to do. I had to keep going.

I couldn't believe I was running. No one more surprised than I. Am I really doing this? I asked myself and then followed it with the reply, YES I AM! For I knew a life alone was far better than a life at my home. Home, how can someone call it that? What is home? Misery? Pain? An endless torture? Why couldn't my mummy be like Lisa's mummy? I hated her. I was jealous of her; of the way her mother took such good care of her.

As I continued to run, I struggled to breathe. I could not take one more breath into my lungs. My lungs, my chest, they hurt, they were hurting real bad. I had to stop again. I bent at the knees and put my hands down onto the ground. I could feel the dirt beneath the grass, dry, smooth, inviting me to lie down. I felt the trickle of more liquid down my cheeks, but it was not blood, not this time. It was salty. I wanted to scream from the bottom of my feet, WHY DID THIS HAVE TO HAPPEN? WHY? Why does it hurt? Why so much! I wanted to scream it louder than the wind.

I wanted the wind to carry that pain and knock over the trees, the fences, all the houses and the people within. I wanted my scream to come bellowing out of my throat, from the passageway that led to the center of my chest. A gale so hard that no one could stand, no not one thing. I wanted to scream it so bad, but I couldn't. It was in me, deep in me, where I stored it, where I swallowed it, deep within my chest. I never wanted to think of that place ever again.

Fearful of what lurked in the dark, I scurried back up onto my feet. I couldn't let them catch me, so I ran across that field again. I didn't know what to do, I didn't know what I was doing, but I knew I couldn't go back, she would kill me. 'Didn't you hear her!' I screamed at myself. 'She will kill you!' This time she'd do it, I knew she would. She hated me more than anything else. She must. What other reason could there be?

The lump in my throat began to grow larger, bulging further from out of my neck. I gulped for air, but it was too much, tears were streaming down my face, I gave up. My eyes were stinging; my legs gave way. I couldn't control it. I couldn't move anymore. I wailed louder than I had ever done before. I sounded like a wounded cat letting out its last screeching whimper before it dies. I fell, unable to control my body any longer. I curled my knees up into my chest and let my head fall to the ground. I stared out into the fog of that night, while pictures of her frothing mouth played through my head, like a movie produced only to haunt me. I could feel the bald patch on the top of my head from where she pulled my hair out. It didn't hurt so much, not amongst the throbbing of my ear. My body started to feel numb. I didn't feel the cold at all. I then began to pray. I began to pray that I never woke up. I knew that if I did, my body would ache and the pain would be unbearable. I prayed to a God that had never answered my prayers; God, whoever you are! I hear people talk about you all the time. They say that you are good and loving too, that you help people, but I don't see this. I don't understand you. I don't know you. You have never helped me. Am I bad? Do you hate me too? Maybe it's true what he said; it's my fault. I am young, I am meant to do what I am told to do. Even if those things feel wrong and hurt me too, I am meant to do what I am told to do. I hate being a girl. I hate being me. I hate me God and I hate you too! Yes I hate you. If you really are who they say you are, then please God, don't let me wake. I don't want to wake up. Please God take me away. I don't want to open my eyes. I do not want to wake.

CHAPTER TWO

DAISY

But of course I did wake up. God did not answer my call. I woke up in that field with the sun beaming down on my face. Everything ached from the bone out. I dragged myself up onto my feet and I promised I would never think of a moment before that one ever again. No moment before existed. I would never talk of what happened and I would never go back. That day I was born again. I was broken, but I was new. Well almost new. My body was mangled and I wondered if there were broken bones too? But I was walking, so I guess that was a good sign.

I found the willow. Turned out it wasn't too far from where I woke. I walked down toward the camp and saw Daisy bent over, rolling up a sleeping bag. She stopped, locked up at me and smiled. She had big brown eyes and long sandy coloured straight hair that looked golden in the light. She looked like the sun had melted into her skin. All she said to me was, 'hey babe, you ready to go?' I nodded and she smiled at me again. It was as if she knew exactly what not to do. Not to ask any questions. I thought for a moment that my wounds weren't really there, that maybe I imagined it all, but then her boyfriend Tom, who was kicking dirt in the fire, looked up at me.

'Jesus! What happened to you!' he exclaimed with his face all scrunched up.

'Leave her alone Tom,' Daisy ordered.

He shook his head and continued to pack their stuff.

I stood true to my word and said nothing about what happened before I woke up. I guess I didn't need to. Half my blonde hair ripped out, bloodstains around my ear. I really was a sorry sight.

I walked down to the dam and began to wash away the salty spots from off my face, left behind by tears. Daisy followed me, dampening a towel and gently patting my head with it. The right side of my head was thumping so badly, I could barely stand the pain.

'You know we can't take her to a doctor, just leave her behind,' Tom called out so that I could hear him too.

'I'm not leaving her behind. She'll be fine. I'll give her some of these.' Daisy pulled out some pills from her bag and gave them to me. 'They'll make you feel better, I promise.' She said it with a smile that made me feel warm inside.

I wondered if other girls had mothers like her. If a part of me hadn't died in the field that night and I hadn't made that promise to never think about my life before that moment, then I would probably have asked myself why my mother wasn't more like her?

'Time to move,' Tom ordered.

Daisy helped me up and walked me to the car.

The next two days were a blur to me, watching roads go by a window. The pills Daisy gave me were strong. I felt no more pain as I drifted in and out of consciousness. Daisy sat in the front seat, the picture of a perfect angel. Her beautiful golden hair hanging loosely on her shoulders, intensified by the light of the sun, as though she was the sole reason for the sun to shine bright. She had holes in her cheeks that came out when she smiled. She told me I was like her; that she was like me. I didn't quite know what she meant. She was older than me. Maybe she meant she had once been me.

Tom (Daisy's boyfriend) was my neighbour's cousin. At least I think they were cousins. I heard him say, 'Cous' so I figured they were related. They were talking about some deal out in the yard and they caught me listening in through the back fence. I wasn't really trying to listen. I was just bored. I got kicked out a lot and would sit in the backyard, so I kind of just heard it. When Tom realised I was there listening to them talk, he jumped the fence and grabbed me by the throat. It didn't shock me, I was used to that. Then Daisy stepped in and calmed him down, so he let me go. The next day she took me to the willow and showed me where they camped. She told me I could come with them if I wanted to, that they were heading to a new town. It was as if she knew my past and she knew what was about to happen. It was as though my story was written in the stars and she knew how to read them.

I wasn't sure how much time had passed by, but when I woke, I woke up on a mattress on the floor. I was somewhere new and the pills had worn off. The room was small and a white sheet covered the window. My ear was still sore but not throbbing as much as before. I wasn't exactly sure how long I had been there. I did feel better, but I was confused. I could hear a distant radio but not from my right ear. I figured the sound would come back after my headache completely disappeared and my wounds had time to heal.

What I thought was a radio in the distance soon turned louder, getting closer and closer to the room that I was laying in and then the noise turned into a scream. Daisy came running into the room and grabbed me by the arm and yanked me toward the door.

'Lets go, now!' she screamed.

Her urgency frightened me but I didn't say a word. I asked no questions. I just followed her outside. We both jumped the fence and I continued to follow her across the neighbouring yard. As we walked out of the driveway and turned down the street, I noticed a deep wound dripping blood from Daisy's arm. She ripped off a piece of her T-shirt and wrapped it around the gash like she had done it many times before.

'Don't worry kiddo, I'll be alright,' and then she flashed me her warming smile.

It was kind of unspoken that we never asked questions. I never asked about all the scars on her arms and legs. I didn't ask about what happened with Tom and she never asked me about what happened before I met her at the willow.

Two months went by and it was just Daisy and I. With no Tom around, Daisy taught me how to survive. She showed me how to get clothes, find shelter and food, as well as how to steal. She was really friendly and easily made deals. As time went by, our tactics would change. Our latest survival trick was to carry a duffle type bag into a department store. We would circle the expensive dresses and gowns, looking out for people that worked there and then quickly, as fast as we could, shove a dress or two in each bag and then run out the door. Daisy had hooked up a pretty sweet deal, one hundred bucks a dress! It was awesome. Well the money was. At the start I was pretty scared and I felt kind of bad, I knew stealing was wrong, but what else was I suppose to do? We were careful and did our best to follow the rule, not to hit the same place twice. One day we made four hundred bucks! So I got used to it and with time it became much easier.

We rarely went hungry and we lived in a squat. There were ten of us sprinkled around four separate rooms. Most of the others were weird but it didn't really matter, we kept to ourselves in our own room.

Daisy would tell me how lucky we were; we had plates, cups and running water too. 'It's better than sleeping on the streets,' she would say, 'you must avoid that at any cost. It's not safe for us.'

I was happy to be with Daisy. I felt safe. It was perfect... but as my life has always gone, the perfect feeling didn't last for very long.

It was a quiet day and the sun was beaming through the yard when I heard the squeal.

'Daisy?' I called out.

Not waiting for an answer, I ran through the empty house to the front door and there was Tom, pinning Daisy up against the wall. He held her by her throat and didn't let her talk. I felt so much rage build up from inside of me, watching him do that to the angel that rescued me. I loved Daisy. She took care of me. How could I let him hurt her again?

I don't know where it came from, but I went up behind Tom and kicked him straight in the balls, right up into his backside. He fell to his knees and Daisy yelled out, 'BACKUP NOW!' I knew what that meant. I was to meet her at the car.

One very important thing Daisy always said, 'you have to have a backup plan.' Ours was fifteen minutes from the squat, down the hill and behind the trees. It was an old car that sat by the electrical plant. Before we found the squat we used to sleep out there. We built fires and sang stupid songs and then locked ourselves in the car at night. She told me then, that if we ever got into trouble that we would head straight back to the car. The code word would be "backup". So I ran like crazy all the way there.

CHAPTER THREE

HAPPY BIRTHDAY

I ran so frantically that I could not catch my breath. Even the night that I escaped, I couldn't remember being that out of breath. I guess it was Daisy. She was my everything; my sister, my teacher, my protector. I had to run. I had to run for her, to protect her too.

When I arrived at the car, Daisy had already plonked herself down on the torn away armchair, dragged there by us, which felt like years ago now. She smiled and giggled and let out a sigh, then stated as though it was common knowledge, 'he always finds me.' She didn't seem worried and I figured this must have happened many times before.

I barely got my words out between puffs of air, but managed to ask her, 'what will he do?'

'He'll calm down, don't worry, he always does this.'

I found it strange that he always does this. Does she always leave him? Does he always hurt her? Why does she go back? These questions kind of made me wish I had asked her about Tom, but then I remembered she had never asked me anything about my past and I never wanted to answer those kinds of questions. It frightened me that he might be back in our lives. Would she do that? Would he stay with us? I didn't trust him and I didn't like him. He never wanted me to come with them. If Daisy hadn't of pushed for me, I could be dead right now. I let that thought shudder off my body. I promised myself to never go back to any moment before that day in the field, before the willow, before Daisy. It did not exist.

We had sat around that old armchair many times before. We would light a fire and paper, scissors, rock, who would get to sleep on the back seat of the car. I'd gotten pretty good at that game. I knew what Daisy would pick and I would win more than lose. We would talk for hours and play cards and then just before we would go to sleep, Daisy would take me through the rules of the street; always have an exit plan, two if possible. Always know where a weapon could be or what you could use. Never sleep on the streets at any cost. Avoid dark alleys, laneways and groups of guys. She said bad things happen to you when you are on your own, so always stick to a group no matter how much you hate them or how they may irritate you. It's about safety in numbers. Once you have a place to sleep, scout the surroundings for the nearest toilets, usually a supermarket, train station or even at the cinemas, then look for a bakery as they always have left over food chucked in their bins.

So I began to gather up some sticks and branches ready to build a fire, just as Daisy had taught me months ago. There was always a can of gasoline by the car. It was weird cause the can always seemed full. I guess we weren't the only ones that used that spot. It certainly was a big help when you were trying to light a fire on a windy day.

Something felt eerie about that night. It was unusually still for that side of the hill. I decided to ignore the odd feeling in my toes, after all it was cold, they were probably just frozen. I tipped a small amount of gasoline onto the pile of wood and grabbed the stash of matches that were kept in the glove box of the car. It was the worst if you had to rub sticks together for hours in the cold air, trying to get a spark.

'Will we be here all night?' I asked Daisy.

Daisy was playing with a stick, prodding the fire.

'It's probably best. We'll just let him calm down.'

Then she gave me a twinkle. It's this smile she does to let me know everything is OK.

'Daisy,' I said, 'I've got something to tell you, something about today.'

'Now what would that be mini scrag?' Tom asked, as he walked over from behind the car.

Startled and afraid I darted toward Daisy, who calmly stood up and moved me behind her, as though to shield me from what was about to happen next.

'Babe, we gotta talk,' Tom directed at Daisy.

'We don't need you anymore Tom,' she responded.

That's right we don't, I thought to myself, agreeing with what Daisy had said. What did she see in him anyway? He looked more sickly than ever before in his torn Adidas tracksuit pants that were too big for his waist. His face sunken in like someone sucked the water out of his body. He was gangly and tall and frightened me with his angry stare.

Tom approached us and I tightened my grip on Daisy's jacket.

'Listen,' he said. 'I just got to talk you D. Alright?'

'I've got nothing to say. Not this time.' Daisy didn't take a step back. She stood her ground.

Then Tom spat out through gritted teeth, 'there's been nothing but trouble since you took that bitch!' He pointed his finger directly at me.

'There's always been nothing but trouble with you!' Daisy growled back.

They continued to spit words of fire back and forth at each other. Tom was a loose cannon. I didn't know if he was going to explode, if I should run, or what I should do? I drew in a breath and started to think back to what Daisy had taught me; the rules of the streets.

Rule one; check for exits. So I bounced my eyes around the paddock and decided the best place to lose him was to squeeze through the electrical plant fence, make my way to the other side and jump over the next fence. That's if I could out run him. Second rule; look for a weapon. Nervously I bit my lip and decided that the gasoline can was the closest. I could grab it and swing it across his head. I had never hurt anyone before and I was scared to do so, but if I had to, then I would.

'Babe, babe, OK, OK...' Tom pleaded, lowering his hands. 'I was wrong, just listen to me babe, I love you babe, babe, I love you, babe.'

And that's how he had her. Every time I imagined. I couldn't believe that jerk was saying he loved her, after everything. After he cut her arm and choked her up against a wall, then saying I love you, I felt sick to my core. I could feel the acid rising up in my throat, as my heart pumped, ready to flee.

Tom reached out his hands to Daisy with puppy dog eyes. I couldn't believe she was falling for it.

'Babe listen to me,' he said as he grabbed her hands, pulling her in. 'I'm in trouble.'

'Not again!' Daisy pulled away.

'Listen babe, listen! It's Cous!'

My stomach fell to the ground as I was taken back to my life before that night in the field.

'It all went wrong babe. Now babe...' he said getting closer. 'You were with me from the start. If he is after me, then he is after you.'

'Shit!' Daisy said under her breath, then she hit him across the chest. 'Why the fuck did you come here then?'

'Look babe, if you hadn't of run out we could of fixed this.'

'You did not just blame me, you fuc...'

Stopping mid word Daisy turned to me, 'give us some time OK Ange?'

I nodded my head and walked away from the camp, having no idea what went on. The deal? Went wrong? What deal? How did it go so wrong? And why was Cous after Daisy? What did she do? The whole no asking questions thing was really bothering me. I felt completely in the dark. The name Cous made me feel sick. It's all from my life before I woke up in that field. All the questions and memories of the past sent a sickly hot liquid from my stomach right up through my neck. I pushed it back down along with all of the memories and told myself, 'there is no life before that night, you hear!'

I walked far away from the camp and sat down next to a large rock, leaning my head against its smooth side. I didn't want to hear anymore. I didn't want to know and I didn't want to remember. I was keeping my promise to myself.

I never did get my hearing back in my right ear (I guess the blows must have burst my eardrum). So I pressed my left ear against that rock and blocked out every sound. For me it was silent and dark.

I must have fallen asleep for when I woke there was commotion, more so than before. It sounded like four or five different muffled voices. I opened my eyes and slowly lifted my head up from off the rock and as soon as I did, the sound came flooding back into my left ear and I realised the muffled voices were in fact screams and pleading.

One guy was holding Daisy by her arms as she cried and screamed for them to stop. Tom was on the ground being beaten by someone I couldn't quite see. There were four of them laughing as a boot came down, kicking Tom in the face. I looked for a weapon. It was dark and hard to see. My eyes locked onto a stick almost as big as me and I decided I had to grab it. As I lent over, one of them called out, 'Cous' and I froze. My breath almost stopped, I could not move. Was my mother there too? What if he knew who I was and took me back to that place of torture? I'd rather die then ever go near that place again.

I wanted to scream out, Daisy what do I do? But I couldn't and I couldn't run because they would see me too. How could I get help without them seeing me? I pleaded to God; please God help them! At that moment Daisy broke free and tried to beat Cous from off of Tom. The youngest one of the group, no older than sixteen, raised a bat and hit Daisy over the head. She fell to the ground heavy and limp. My eyes, my chest, my whole being was bursting with tears, yet I had to suck them in. I had to contain them in fear of being heard.

Cous then took the bat from the young ones hands and whacked Tom across the head, not once but twice. It was the most chilling sound that echoed across the hill, a sound I would never forget. There was no movement from Daisy nor Tom.

They continued to laugh and spat at their bodies before dragging them into the car. They emptied the can of gasoline and lit up a match; it was Cous that flicked it that started the blaze.

I stood frozen as they took off into the night, my head spinning out of control. Not one single sound came out of me. Not a blink of an eye nor a breath or a sob, I felt nothing. My body had been emptied. There was nothing of me left. I just lost the one person who ever cared about me and there was nothing I could do. No police to call for they would send me home to die, but I already felt dead.

I never got to tell her that something that I had to say. I was going to tell her that it was my thirteenth birthday that day.

CHAPTER FOUR

WHAT NEXT

I never thought it was possible to hate anything more than I hated my life from before that night in the field, but I found it. I hated myself. I hated myself more than anything else in the world. I wondered for days, not knowing what next to do or where to go. I couldn't risk staying at the squat. What if Cous was looking for me? What if he knew who I was? And what if the others in the squat knew I did nothing to help Daisy and then beat me to a pulp? No, I knew I couldn't stay there, but after a day I was tired and hungry. The best plan I could come up with, was to hide across the road from the squat and wait for everyone to leave. I watched for a whole day and night, counting how many people went in and out. When I was sure it was empty, I ran through the house as quick as I could, gathering only essentials. I didn't stop to look for any clues to see if they knew what was going on and I didn't go near her things. I couldn't bring myself to touch them. I left as quickly as I entered and ran all the way to the station. All I could think about was getting far, far away, where nobody knew me. Where no one had seen me before.

Daisy had told me about her life in Sydney, where she grew up, where she ran to and where she stayed. I decided to head there. I would be safe. There would be loads of streeties around. That's what she used to call them, call us (the homeless); streeties. I guess it fit just as good as any other name. I missed her. It was all my fault.

I thought arriving in Sydney would be much grander than it was. Grander? Is that a word? I guess I mean more wow. Not that I had been to a big city before, I just expected it to be different. More scary maybe.

When I got off the train at Central Station it was almost lunchtime and I hadn't eaten in a while. I had no more money so I wasn't really sure what I was going to do. I probably would have asked the question to God. Something like, 'God what do I do now?' But I think I proved my point that he does not exist. It's a topic I will no longer discuss.

Kings Cross was the place where Daisy had been, so I knew that it was there that I should go, but first I wanted to see the bridge. I'd heard about it many times but had no idea where it was. So I began to just walk.

It's funny how people can see right through you. I know they're just ignoring me, but it feels as though you don't exist. I was pretty small and scrawny too, matted blonde hair that hadn't been brushed since... I don't know. I could not remember. I really did need a shower. It had been quite a few days. I thought about how hard it was going to be to find a squat, but I figured there must be loads, cause there's so many more people in Sydney.

I followed George Street right through the middle of the city, stopping to look at the giant shops. So many pretty dresses. I wondered how hard it would be to shove one in my bag? Probably no point though, I didn't know anyone I could sell them too.

I came across this amazing ice-cream shop, with about fifty different flavours! It looked so good and I wanted one really bad. Three flavours at least! I must have been staring for a while lost in my own world, cause some girls laughed at me, then pushed me out the way. They said how bad I smelt and laughed in my face. It made me miss Daisy even more.

I decided the bridge could wait for another day. I didn't feel much like looking at it any more.

'Excuse me, do you know which direction to Kings Cross?' I must have asked twenty people, all who ignored me but one. An old lady with a brown funny hat who asked me, 'are you lost child?' to which I replied, 'yes.' I knew better than to tell the truth and told her, 'my mother is waiting for me there.' The last thing I wanted was for her to tell the police I was on my own and send me back to that hellhole. No, I thought if I had survived this far then I could keep going on my own. I didn't think it could get any worse.

I followed the brown hat lady's directions and found myself staring up at a gigantic coke sign. It was massive! I stood there for ages, not realising the time, for I had no clue what to do next. A lump started to rise in my throat and I crossed my arms and held my breath, determined not to cry. But it all got too much, as the realisation set in that I was alone. I turned and ran down the first street I saw, throwing myself against a brick wall. I sobbed into my jacket, trying to muffle the sound. All I could think was that I had nowhere to go. I opened my eyes, but could see nothing; the colours were all grey. It was a cloudy sky with limited light and my eyes were full of tears. It all looked like a blur. A big grey blur. I curled up on the ground amongst the piled up rubbish and asked myself, is this even a street? I couldn't tell. I had no idea if I was in an alley or in the middle of a busy road. All reason and rules went out the window, my brain completely switched off. Emotion had taken me over and clouded my brain. It was so completely stupid of me (after everything Daisy had taught me), I was going against rule number three in that very moment; avoid dark alleys and laneways. Rule one also broken; make sure you have at least two clear exits, three or four is better. Rule four gone; never leave yourself alone, always be fully aware of your surroundings and who is sharing that space. NEVER LEAVE YOURSELF

ALONE. Rule two; weapon. I couldn't see through the tears, but I felt a hand tap me on the shoulder, snapping me back into reality and flooding my head with all of Daisy's words.

I stood up realising I was alone in a dark alley with a man standing beside me.

CHAPTER FIVE

THE PIMP

It was hard for me to remember what school was like. I did have friends. Some of them were lots of fun, but I never really trusted anyone. We were always fighting for this one girls attention. We all feared her but we all wanted to be her best friend. We wanted to be popular.

I remember in grade three, I had this friend Abigail, strange name really, but Abigail was my friend. We hung out, we'd been to each other's houses and she used to make me laugh. Then one day at school, we were sitting on the carpet in our classroom. Abigail and me were in our usual spot, right up the front near the teacher. Then something miraculous happened. The two coolest girls selected me and another girl called Lisa, to go and sit against the wall at the back of the class with them. So on our bums using both our hands, we maneuvered our butts inch by inch across the carpet, toward the back of the room. We could hardly contain our excitement! We were chosen! They wanted us! Lisa and me... we were in! It felt so good to be wanted and to be liked. I caught a glimpse of Lisa's face and she was smiling just like me.

We slowed down our scooting toward the back, as we didn't want to look too eager. Then the dreaded happened. Abigail started to inch back too! The cool girls yelled out, 'No! Not you! We don't want you here. Go back up the front where you belong with the other geeks.' Abigail's face was so sad. She looked at me and asked me with her eyes, 'stand up for me. Why won't you take me too?' I felt her rejection filling up inside the space in the middle of my chest, but I said nothing. I gulped down our friendship and her welling tears, into the pit of my stomach. I continued to inch back leaving her on her own embarrassed. The feeling of guilt swelled up inside me, churning in my tummy, struggling to stay down. I left her down there at the front of the class, alone and ashamed. Who was she going to sit with now? I felt so horrible. My whole being kind of inward wrapped itself into the back of my body. I knew it was wrong, but this was my chance, somebody actually wanted me. Me! They wanted me and I wasn't going to let that go. Somebody actually wanted me.

Crouched down in that clouded alleyway in the back of Kings Cross, I looked up and saw a slim man. He didn't look mean. He was smiling, asking me if I was OK? He pulled out his phone and offered to call one of my friends to come and get me. I thought to myself, maybe I could trust this person, this man? I wasn't sure how old he was, maybe twenty, he could have even been thirty. I was never really good at guessing peoples ages. I did however wonder why he wore so much jewelry? Seemed kind of odd for a guy.

'Um I don't know anyone here,' I replied.

I should have realised in that moment, once those words left my mouth, that there was something odd with the smirk that spread across his face, but hey what did I know? I was in a foreign city, A CITY, THE BIG SMOKE for Christ sake (not that I believed in God), but hey for God's sake what was I suppose to do?

He took me by the hand. Eweh! His hand was slimy, sweaty, wet, with weird long lady like fingers. He rubbed my hand kind of creepily. 'We have a place for girls like you. You know those who don't have a place to stay or any friends in town. You will like it there, I just know you will.'

Back then I had no idea what instincts were, but if I did, I would have known that the knot in my stomach was not because I hadn't eaten nor was it because I had been balling my eyes out. I would have realised that this man was totally Dodge City and I would have kicked him in the balls and run for it! But I was only just thirteen, with no sense or clue at all, left in the wilderness to fend for myself, to fight any wilder beast that came my way. But this beast was not a typical beast and he was not going to play fair. I had no skills. I wasn't a warrior able to defend my tribe. I had not been taught the art of a single shot with a bow and arrow; I was just a young girl. I was alone in the wilderness, standing in an alley with a man, who was more like a giant meerkat than a beast, leading me toward "accommodation" that he said was, 'impeccably decorated and filled with lovely ladies,' just like myself, even though I was no lady, but merely a teenage girl.

I remember standing at the bottom of a staircase. It was old, stony and grey. I'm not quite sure how else to describe those old stone steps that crept up eerily toward a brown rotten door. It was like some kind of illusion, similar to the 2D pictures, which really became 3D if you stare long and hard enough, going cross-eyed in the meantime. I was being fooled into believing that this was heaven, when in actual fact it was hell. The staircase may have pointed up and not down, but I was definitely walking straight into some kind of hell.

The meerkat slimeball man placed his ladyfingers on my shoulders, slightly bending his fingertips into the top of my breastbone. A sinking feeling immediately filled my stomach. Another instinct moment. If I had of actually known what instincts were, then this was sign number two. Kick him in the balls and run; but I didn't. The sick in my stomach filled right up into the back of my throat and reminded me of that night I ran into that field. My breath started to shorten and I could feel the panic in my head thumping in my heart. It was as if he knew that panic had set in and pushed me through the front door, leading me down the hallway and toward the back room.

The hall seemed to go on forever, like it had no end. Rusted rims where the walls met the carpet, patterned with weird red boxes that almost jumped out at you, as if to say, 'all the diseases in the world are contained right here in this spot,' and then multiplied and projected into a thousand squares all running down a line toward the end of the hall. The smell was a distinct taste of ash, just like my step dads breath, mixed with mouldy sandwiches that had been in the bottom of my school bag for days. My mother used to send me to school with vegemite spread on mouldy bread. I hated vegemite and she knew I did, but she continued to give it to me anyway. I was always too embarrassed to bring my sandwich out at lunchtime, in case the other kids at school saw the green spots on my bread. I was so jealous of everyone else. I wanted their fresh soft white bread lined with lettuce, cheese, tomato and all kinds of salad stuff. I would leave my sandwiches in the bottom of my bag and sometimes forget to take them out. They would grow more mould and have this kind of smoggy smell, like socks that have sat wet and dried in the corner of a room. Yuck! And that is what this place smelt like. It was like I was standing in my school bag with mouldy sandwiches hidden beneath the bottom of the plastic base, but in this case they were hidden in the rusted edged carpet.

We passed by one door, two doors, the third door slightly open. A girl lying still on a bed. I saw her breasts. She was covered loosely by a blanket, her arm hanging heavy by the side of the bed with a needle hanging out of it. OH SHIT! Ran through my head and in that moment I knew I was never getting out of there alive.

I don't know why I do this, but as soon as I panic and my life turns to shit, I search for God, the savior, the one who is going to rescue me. The one who will jump out from behind the curtain and save me. The one who will take me home to a white picket fence and a beautiful mother with curly brown hair, who would smile at me as she opened the door. Her eyes lighting up as I drew closer, wiping her hands on her apron, gesturing for me to come inside, for she has just baked fresh bread and a pot is bubbling on the stove filled with warm milk and honey.

BAM! I was shocked back into reality as the meerkat slimeball man threw me to the floor.

'It's time to get comfortable,' he said. 'Don't worry, I'll take good care of you.'

And with that he loosened his belt and terror waved over me. I could not move. I was stuck. I was frozen. The rules Daisy taught me circled around in my head. Rule one; exit! Try to find at least two. Rule two; weapons! What can you use? What could I use?

I couldn't move. I was frozen. God help me, God please!

The meerkat moved toward the shelf, picking up a needle and placing it in his mouth. He grabbed a spoon and emptied something on it. It was almost grey in colour. He lit under the spoon with a lighter. Is it drugs? I asked myself. Is that what was wrong with that girl in the bed? Did they inject her with drugs? Will he inject me with drugs? Everything at once flashed before my eyes and all I could see was death. I don't want to die! I want to see Daisy. Daisy where are you? I screamed so loud internally, that if a single noise actually left my mouth it would have shattered glass. D A I S Y! I bellowed from out of my heart and into the atmosphere, SAVE ME!

Point zero one of a second later, a deep voice from outside of the door screeched out, 'RAID RAID!' The meerkat dropped the spoon and raced up the hallway toward the yelling voice.

In true miracle sense, I was unfrozen, switched on, circling the room, searching for a way out. This was my chance. I slammed the door, my eyes darting across the room. A window? Behind me! I yanked the black material draped across it as hard as I could, tearing it from the secured nails above. I saw a latch and pulled it hard and pushed the glass up with all of the strength I had. I heard thumps down the hallway that could only be the sound of running feet. My heart started pumping out of my sides, my back, my throat and the pit of my stomach. It was as though my heart all at once had nowhere and everywhere to go. I could hear yelling through the door and pushed myself to go. Don't look, don't hesitate, don't even consider, just jump I said to myself. JUMP! And with that I threw my legs out over the ledge and let my body follow to the ground below.

CHAPTER SIX

RUNNING

Clawing at the concrete I scurried to my feet. I don't think I even blinked. I don't remember how I jumped the fence nor who was behind me or what was happening in that house. I had never been more scared in my life... frightened to my very core. Pounding one foot in front of the other, not knowing where I was, where I was going or who was going to catch me? If the police got me, then I'd be back to where I was before that night in the field and I could never let that happen. But if that man caught me, if he found me, then I wouldn't want to live at all.

One, two, three minutes later? Heck I don't know. It could have been only thirty seconds or even ten minutes later, but I still hadn't stopped. I didn't see faces or cars, just fence after fence. Turning a corner I slipped, sliding into first base, skidding my knee along a concreted floor, my foot pushed through the bottom of a gate. Half in the street and half through the gate, I pulled up my knee to inspect the graze. It stung. Little rocks and dirt embedded in my flesh, it started to bleed. I felt helpless and stupid. I wanted to cry, but first I needed somewhere safe, somewhere sheltered from the open streets. I pushed the gate all the way open and pulled myself up against the fence. Thank God! I thought as I noticed a blue painted shed with no locks on the door, sitting in the corner of that little backyard. I barged my way into the shed and shut the metal door behind me.

As I lowered myself to the ground, reality sank in and salty liquid began to run down my cheeks. Hello old friend, I said to my tears, haven't we been here before? Just a few hours ago? I questioned if this was a never-ending cycle, these tears. Would they always stream down my face? Would there always be a new tragedy to cry over? Would the sadness ever go away? I was trying to distract myself from thinking about what had just happened, to stop the flow of tears. I found one distraction by asking myself, why do I say thank God? Thank God for what? For putting me in this situation? For giving me a screwed up life full of pain and misery? I wondered what I would say to God if I saw him? Maybe, 'fuck you, I hate you too.' For it wasn't God who helped me in that moment when I screamed out internally for help. It was Daisy. I screamed her name. It was as though she was still protecting me from somewhere else. It was literally point zero one of a second later that guy screamed raid. What would have happened to me Daisy? What the hell did just happen to me? What did

I just escape from? Actually, I didn't want to know. I didn't want to know why he unbuckled his pants. I didn't want to know what was on the spoon and I didn't want to know what happened to that girl in the other room. I never wanted to think of that place ever again. I thought to myself, that maybe that day, could be just like the day in the field. It never existed, just like most of my life.

I curled up on the floor and prayed again that I did not wake and that if I did wake, I prayed that I would wake anew and nothing from that day had happened. I drifted off into that dreamlike state, where you are still awake but almost asleep. I couldn't help but hate myself. I should have known that when someone wanted me, it always came with a price. Those who want me, want to harm me, so I didn't want to be wanted ever again.

In the last second, before the darkness sent me to sleep, I thanked Daisy.

'Daisy, thank you.'

When I woke up, it felt like I had been asleep for days. I guess that crazy rage of intense adrenaline will do that to you. Completely drain you of all your energy. I felt zapped, tired and weak. The sun had just risen and I knew it was time to leave the shed.

I took a quiet walk around the house, thinking I might find something of value, something I could use or sell. It was pretty obvious no one was home from the overflowing mailbox and the flashing answering machine that I could clearly see through the kitchen window. I realised pretty quickly they were on vacation, which meant I could finally have a shower! Oh my God... I mean oh hurray! (I had to stop using that God word).

I was filled with excitement, with the possibility of a hot shower. I took a minute to pause, as I imagined me sitting on the shower floor letting the warm water build up around me. Maybe I'd even wash my hair! Don't go too crazy Ange, I smiled to myself, I wouldn't be able to wash the soap out of my dreaded mop! Excitedly, I'd still give it a go.

I remember my first time breaking into a house. You'd think it'd be scary but it was kinda funny and pretty easy. Daisy and me walked up and down this same street for about a week. In the morning we saw what time people went to work, what time they came home and who lived at the house. It wasn't rocket science. On a street with no kids, it was empty pretty much the whole day. You just gotta watch out for the oldies. There was this one house with a yard that had no dog, no kids and a kitchen window that was left open every day. How stupid were they! The only thing we had to watch out for was the old lady who lived next door. We knew for sure she was nosey. So Daisy had a look in the old lady's letterbox, noted her name and waited for her to be out in the garden.

'What are you doing?' I asked Daisy.

'Shhh, just follow my lead, wait by the back door. Stay out of sight.'

I did as I was told and watched Daisy walk up along the back fence and yell out, 'hi Mrs. Myrtle, my uncle left a key for me under the back door mat.'

'OK child,' the voice on the other side of the fence muffled back.

Wow, really? I thought. She was real risky Daisy, but she also had one of those smiles that everybody trusted. She looked like she wouldn't hurt a flea. She was actually pretty clever, cause if that lady was going to bust us, she would have said straight away, 'he has no niece. What did you say your name was?' Then we would have to flee. But this way, we knew if we made a noise or the old lady saw a shadow, she wouldn't call the cops straight away.

You can actually break into a house pretty quietly, especially through an open window. Daisy used to say to me, 'you don't have to be the best at something, just smarter at it than everyone else.' She was always right. We only took what we needed, food for the journey and any loose change we could find. Nine times out of ten, I bet no one even noticed that we had been in there. Daisy always said that breaking in was the last resort, to be done only for supplies when starving and before moving on to a different area. We mostly stole food from supermarkets because it was easy and that way we didn't need to break into people's places all that often. Daisy was pretty serious about staying away from cops. I guess she was running from a past she didn't want anyone to know about either.

So just as Daisy had taught me, I circled the house and looked for sensor lights, but there were none, so I knew they had no alarm system. Then I searched the garden, under pot plants, doormats and in the shed. I scanned the back door and noticed a very old teapot sitting at the bottom of the stairs and inside it was the spare key! I wondered if I could still get arrested for letting myself in with a key? It's not the same as kicking in a window or breaking down the door. I was simply letting myself in. It's not exactly "breaking in" now is it?

I unlocked the backdoor with barely a sound and pushed the door open very quietly. I walked into the kitchen which was cluttered, filled with old kettles and teapots of all sorts of strange sizes. Some with bright loud patterns and others were sprouting tiny little trees. The breakfast table was piled high with paper and crap. Six plain wooden chairs surrounded it and a baby's highchair sat in the corner. I wondered how big their family was? My question immediately answered by the hundreds of pictures scattered across the fridge door. There was a woman smiling with golden blonde hair. It looked silky and soft to touch. She had her arms wrapped around two young girls, smiling proudly. She was happy. I thought about how she probably baked for her kids and made them yummy dinners every night. My stomach rumbled at the thought of dinner and I closed my eyes tight, wishing for some delicious white bread and butter to be on the other side of the fridge door. I reached out and opened it up. Oh glorious food! I had to take a step back. I was overwhelmed by the choices that were right in front of me. My tummy skipped as though it was celebrating by jumping a mini rope. A rush of excitement whooshed through me and my stomach screamed, 'feed me!' Without a second to wait, I got stuck in. Cheese! Yum! I love cheese. There was also some weird meat thing, so I passed on that. But then there was Jam! Butter! Bread? Where was the bread? I opened the freezer door, finding exactly what I was looking for. Thank you... (This time stopping myself from saying the G word, cause we know how ridiculous that is). Hmmmm bread. Sweet, sweet toast how I love you so. Toast with butter and jam. All I could think was, how good is life right now! How easily I forgot everything that had just happened to me. I felt happy in that moment.

It's funny how one minute you can feel so hungry, that the whole world might end and your stomach just might eat you up from the inside out, to then eating so much food that you totally feel full, bent over in pain but so bloody happy that you ate. I love food!

I rubbed my belly in a food coma style and stared back at the pictures on the fridge door. One of the girls looked about eleven or ten years old. She could have been fifteen, I wasn't sure. I really was bad at guessing ages. I wondered if those girls lived in that house? I imagined that their mum, the blonde haired woman, would make them hot breakfast in the morning. She would brush their hair then pull it back into a ponytail, kiss them on the check and say, 'come on dears, it's time for me to drive you to school.' I imagined she would hand them a brown paper bag containing fresh white bread salad sandwiches, then she would hold their hands and walk them out the door.

I sighed heavily, not knowing why I did. Why do I imagine other people's lives to be so perfect? It didn't make me feel any good. I guess maybe I just always dreamed of that for myself but couldn't put me in the picture. I mean look at me, as if I could ever have that.

I looked down at my gross clothes that had not been changed for over a week and I slowly began to smile as I realised, FRESH CLOTHES!!!! If those girls lived there, then I could have new clothes! Maybe a jacket or a woolen jumper. I could have a whole backpack full of stuff. And just like that, I took off like a kid who'd just been told where all the Easter eggs are on a hunt. I sprinted up the stairs to the top floor, dancing through the corridor and into one of the rooms. I threw myself onto the bed, giggling and kicking with excitement. I had just hit the jackpot!

'OK, OK, OK,' I said to myself. I needed to calm down. First I had to shower.

So I went into the bathroom and turned on the hot tap. As I stepped into the shower, it felt like I was being hugged by rainbows. So warm, so soft. It was magical. It was blissful. I even washed my hair. It had been a really long time. It was pretty hard to get all of the soap out, but I think I got it all. My hair had become so matted and tangled, I was starting to form dreadlocks.

My blissful state was interrupted by a noise downstairs and I immediately had that sinking feeling in the bottom of my feet again as my stomach hit the floor. I leaped out of the shower and straight into the bedroom, hoping the owners had not come home. Like a record on repeat, I said to myself, 'damn it Ange, why did you get so comfortable?'

I found some fresh undies, jeans, a T-shirt, a jumper and jacket. I put them on as fast as I could and tried to calm myself down. Maybe I was just being paranoid. Still I needed an exit strategy just in case.

I tiptoed down the staircase and heard a noise by the back door. Did I lock it? I couldn't remember. There were muffled sounds and then some glass breaking on the floor. Then I knew it was definitely time for me to split. But before I could run, a hand grabbed my right arm and another grabbed my left. I screamed, 'let me go! I didn't take anything!'

A scruffy man, lanky and unshaven, came running in with a boy about the same age as me.

'What the bloody hell?' Scruffy man blurted out.

As though realising the situation we were all in, scruffy man lowered his voice and said, 'cover her mouth you two.'

You two who? Who was he talking about? I turned my head and my attackers were two kids; a girl and a boy. They looked a little younger than me and so I struggled free. Remembering rule two; weapon, I grabbed a chair and waved it around, using it like a bull guy uses that red cloth thing.

'All right little girl,' scruffy dude said in a lowered tone. 'It's OK. No one needs to get hurt, just don't scream. We just want to talk to your mummy, that's all.'

'Mummy?' I don't have a mother, rang through my head. I was confused until I realised, he must have been thinking that it was my house. 'This isn't my house,' I said, still clutching the chair.

The scruffy man laughed in a mumbled way. I thought he must have been mad or crazy or something. We all looked at him confused.

'Ah kids. She's breaking in just like us!'

'Oh,' 'ah,' 'what do we do now?' they asked.

'Well me love,' the scruffy man said as he scratched his beard. 'This is ours, so you need to leave.'

A sound then rang out, one we were all too familiar with. The bleeping of a siren and the flashing of blue and red lights.

'SPLIT! SAFETY POINT!' yelled the scruffy man.

Everyone dropped whatever they were holding, my chair included. We all headed for the backdoor and bolted out of the back gate, through the back street and sure enough I was running again.

All four of the others started to split up, which left me unsure about what to do. They headed in different directions. I was scared to go on my own and I didn't want to be alone, after all it was rule number four; never leave yourself alone. So I decided to follow the youngest boy who had been holding my left arm. I was just as fast as he was and I caught up to him in no time. He didn't look back toward me. I don't think he even noticed that I was there. I convinced myself that he also needed a friend, that maybe I could be his. After all he looked so young, much younger than me.

CHAPTER SEVEN

THE OTHERS

Bent over and out of breath, we crouched down by the back door of a 7-Eleven store. Between puffs of air the boy managed to ask me, 'what are you doing here?'

'I've got nowhere else to go,' I replied.

At that moment, one by one, the other three arrived.

Like a rooster crowing, the scruffy man let out a, 'woo hoo, feel that rush!'

I really did think he was a bit mad.

He held out his hand and introduced himself, 'I'm Dave.'

Apprehensively, I shook his hand and told him my name was Ange. I'm not quite sure why I was so apprehensive? I guess odd-looking men kind of scared me now. I convinced myself he must be all right, I mean, there were three other kids with him. I decided to ignore the odd feeling in my toes and put it down to all that running we just did.

Dave actually reminded me of a teacher I once had. He was bubbly with bouncy curls on the top of his head. In fact, if it wasn't for the curls, I reckon you'd mistake him for that guy in the cartoon Shaggy. You know the dude with Shaggy the dog? Or is he called Shaggy and the dog called Doo? Shaggy Doo? I don't know. I wasn't allowed to watch cartoons in the mornings like everyone else at school. It was at Abigail's house that I saw those episodes. It was a pretty funny show. I hadn't thought about Abigail in a while, I still felt pretty bad about ditching her in school that day. Fat load of good it did me, ditching her like that. I don't ever want to treat anyone like that ever again. I decided I wouldn't hurt anyone and even promised myself, if I was to get through all of this, that I was going to help other girls like me... one day.

'Hey you? Earth to homeless girl?'

I pushed the clicking fingers away from out of my face. 'I'm Jase,' he said, 'and this is Lena and Mike.' He pointed to the two younger kids.

Two little hello's came out of their mouths, with cute little smiles too. They seemed shy, but not like newbies to the streets. From the way that they grabbed me in that house, I knew they'd been on the streets for a while. They had done that before. It was like a routine. They knew the drill. It was a sequence they practiced regularly. I understood that. You need to have an out, a safety word, a thing that you do, something planned in case you get into trouble. They were lucky they had four of them. You just never know who might jump you. Daisy used to say to me, 'if only you knew Ange, but you're too precious to tell. One day I will.'

'So which squat you at?' Jase asked me.

'I don't have one. I don't know anyone here.'

'Well,' interrupted Dave, 'we've got space for one more. We could use the extra hands, gather some food, beg on the streets. Yeah we'll get good use out of you.'

No one argued with him. He put his arm around my shoulder and squeezed me in a couple of times. 'Well let's go,' he said.

I hate people touching me. Get your arm off me! I was saying in my head. It's like I get paralysed each time it happens and I don't say what I'm really feeling, which is DON'T TOUCH ME. I sometimes jump when someone only slightly touches me. It could be so small, but by my reaction it would seem like they just hit me with a hammer I jump so high. But this time, I definitely did not say anything. I wouldn't dare. I needed somewhere to sleep, somewhere, where someone else could take watch. Daisy and I used to do that. I would stay awake while she slept and then she would do the same for me. It was her rule. 'Just in case,' she would say and then she'd smile at me. I missed her, but I dared not think of her. Every time I did, I slumped a little lower into my body, as I buried the grief further down below my heart. There wasn't much space left in there anymore cause it was full with tears, but I wasn't going to let myself feel them, not then, not in front of those new people.

They had a pretty good setup. Don't get me wrong, the place was a dump, but it had a roof, minimal damage and running water too. The place had been left years ago. Graffiti everywhere, boards up on most of the windows except the standard two or three exits, just in case of an emergency; the quick getaway. Streeties had clearly been through there before. I could tell by the burn marks on the floor. How else do you stay warm in winter? Best way is to burn tin bins filled with branches and wood. It always leaves a mark on the floor, but it'll keep you warm. I was surprised that some of those fires didn't burn the whole place down. I guess no one worried about that. If you burnt it down, then you probably did the owners a favour. This particular place stunk like piss, but still I was grateful.

'There's plenty of blankets and stuff in there, we've got our own sleeping bags...' Scruffy said and then looked at me, 'doesn't look like you have anything at all?'

I nodded back. I didn't have anything at all.

'My room's in there,' he pointed and I am sure he winked at me too. Creep. 'The kitchen is here. As you can see supremo!' He chuckled and continued out the back.

The kitchen was disgusting. Mould so bad it was black and growing up the cupboard doors. With missing boards in the floor, I carefully stepped over the holes, pulling my jacket up over my nose to block out the smell. It shuddered memories of mouldy sandwich schoolbags and scary meerkat hallways through my brain.

'We keep food in here. A little more sanitary, don't you think?' Scruffy smiled and winked at me again. Don't you think winking is creepy? I do.

We walked through the laundry, which was also the food pantry, and out the backdoor onto the decking.

'We're pretty covered here,' he pointed out to the trees by the fence. 'For safety sake, don't spend too much time out here. You are expected to pull your weight, do food runs, bring in some dollars and even watch the other two, especially Lena. Other than that, come and go as you please but only when it's dark. Don't bring anyone back here and make sure you don't get seen. Questions?'

I shook my head no.

'Good. I'll get Jase to take you out for a run.'

And no, it wasn't the exercise kind of run. It was begging, stealing and bread. A whole new set of rules, a whole new list of things to do. Their rules. I didn't like it so much. I wondered if Daisy would be ok with it? Still it was good for me not to be alone and Lena was cool. She was real cute and nice. Yeah it was good to have Lena around.

CHAPTER EIGHT

LENA

Lena was cute. Big brown eyes like her brother. I worked it out pretty quickly that Jase was her older brother. They never told me why they were on the streets. I knew better than to ask about mothers and fathers, after all I didn't want to share my story. I knew that whatever it was they ran away from, must have been really bad. Nobody chooses this life. No one wants to live like this. None of us do, but this is better than what we had at home. Must have been pretty bad huh? For some of us, it was too late to turn back.

'Angie,' the sweet little Lena voice whispered.

'Yes?'

'Will you go out and play with me?'

Lena was younger than me, eleven. Somehow she had been hidden from the police and from anyone that could take her away. It's easier when you are thirteen or fourteen and maybe you could pass for being as old as sixteen, nobody asks questions. In fact people seemed to be really afraid of us. Seems pretty stupid, we're just kids. The problem with Lena, she looked like she was seven, so we couldn't let her out after dark. It just looked too suss.

'How about we go tomorrow? In the morning?'

She twisted and turned on her feet, looking at me with her big brown eyes. She was just so cute it was so hard to say no.

'But,' she said, twirling my matted blonde hair in her fingers, 'the others aren't even here. We could be back before they arrive, it's only like five o'clock.'

I bit my lip a little unsure what to do. She was bored and I didn't blame her. I was bored too sitting in that dingy old house.

'Come on Angieeeeee,' she said, drawing out the e, emphasising her cuteness, 'it stinks in here.'

I pressed my nose to hers and looked into those big brown eyes and said, 'you're right it stinks in here. Come on let's go.'

I knew it was wrong to leave the house, they trusted me to watch her. It had only been a week and I didn't want to rock the boat. But instead of listening to that voice inside, I grabbed Lena's hand, pulled myself up onto my feet and we skipped toward the door. The door was jammed again and I had to give it a good kick. I jiggled the lock and pulled the handle and finally we were out, running across the road and toward the park. Not sure why we battled with that door every single time, when the window to the left had no glass and was wide open; our emergency exit.

When we got to the park, we threw our arms out wide and flew around like aeroplanes. We giggled like little birds that had just grown their very first wings. 'Wooooooooo,' I swept in and tickled Lena under the arms. We fell to the ground laughing and rolling around, trying to see who can tickle the other the most.

A sudden stomp on my wrist, sent pain shooting up my arm. I screamed out, 'hey! Arhhhh!'

'What the fuck are you doing here?'

It was Jase! I jumped up onto my feet.

'Lena wanted to play and...'

Jase cut me off, grabbing me, pulling me by my wrist. 'You know she can't be out!' he barked at me.

Lena jumped up and pulled at her brothers arm, 'leave her alone. J! Leave her alone!'

Throwing my hand away, Jase grabbed Lena and pushed her toward the road, 'now go!'

'But J,' pleaded Lena.

'Go!'

I grabbed Lena's hand and walked her speedily back toward the house. I gave her a little comforting smile, then turned back and looked over my shoulder. Jase was walking back toward a group of guys over by the slide. I'd seen them before. Two days ago, when it was my turn to hit the back of the bakery for the end of day throw outs, I saw them do a drug deal. They beat some guy up and took off with his money. Now Jase was in the park doing some weird handshake with them. He knew them. Rule number five; no gangs, it was the kind of trouble that would get you in jail or worse, sent home.

It was later that night I knew something was about to turn. Jase took Lena away and wouldn't let her come near me. In fact, I think he said something to her about me, cause she didn't want to talk to me anymore. But it wasn't that, that concerned me. It was Dave. I caught him staring at me. It sent a shiver down my spine. Something inside said to me, don't be alone with him.

CHAPTER NINE

THE CLOTHES BIN

It was my turn to hit the bakery at the back of Kellett Way. At the end of the day, they'd leave all the unsold bread, pies, cakes, whatever's left over, out on the back step. Pretty good of them hey, leaving all that stuff out for the streeties. We hadn't starved yet, although sometimes it was a shit fight, cause everybody wanted the cakes.

'I'm heading out to the bakery,' I called out.

No one responded. Lena and Mike were throwing a bouncy ball against the wall at each other. They didn't turn around, just continued to ignore me.

'Fine,' I sighed. Whatever. With all the crap and silent treatment, I didn't want to be there anymore.

'I'll come with you, we could walk together,' Dave called out from the other room.

As fast as he said it, I slid out the front window. The last thing I wanted was for him to come with me. The staring at me was creeping me out and getting worse. I was defo not going to walk with him.

Everything seemed pretty normal that day. Same street, same shops, same back streets. I knew my way round pretty good. It was a boring walk and I kind of wished Lena could walk with me, but it was almost dark and well, who knows what Jase said to her, she hadn't even looked at me since I took her to the park. I decided to walk around to the front of the bakery cause out the back was not exactly the kind of spot you wanted to get stuck alone. I was pretty good at scoping things out. I could read if it was safe or not, but since the meerkat incident I was sticking to rule number three; avoid dark alleys, laneways and groups of guys.

I approached the side of the building and took a step back. Is that Jase? I asked myself, as he fondled a bag full of pills. No wait, not pills, a white grey-ish lumpy stuff. It was like the stuff on the spoon in that hellhole meerkat house. My shoulders shook just thinking about it.

What the hell was Jase doing? I leaned forward trying to work it all out... then shit! He saw me. I moved off quickly toward the front of the shop but he grabbed me and pinned me up against the wall.

'Let go of me Jase!'

'What the hell are you doing snooping around?'

'I'm here for the bread, it's left over time.'

His face was way too close to mine. I hated being that close to anyone.

'Get off me!'

I used my forearm to push him away, which only made him more angry.

He pushed me back against the wall and I could feel his breath on the side of my cheek.

'What did you say?'

Not making any eye contact at all I gritted my teeth and confronted him, 'I saw you doing a drug deal. Does Lena...'

He shoved me hard against the wall and punched me in the stomach. I immediately dropped to the ground unable to breathe. It felt like my stomach fell out of my back.

He leaned down and grabbed a handful of my hair. 'You'll say nothing.' Then he let me go with a forceful push. I didn't wait around for round number two. I knew the drill; two exits, a weapon and if all else fails, run. I ran.

When I reached the house, I didn't go in. I needed a minute to gather my thoughts. It was as though scruffy Dave was waiting for me and came sliding out of the back door.

'No bread huh? So many kids round here all got wind of that bakery. No matter we still got some from yesterday.'

He leaned against the door and gestured for me to come over. That was definitely my cue to get out of dodge. I made my way to the door, but he grabbed my hand and pulled me toward him.

'I'm going inside,' I said, trying to shake my hand free but he only gripped it tighter.

He moved closer toward me, grabbing my waist and pulling me in closer to his body. 'I know you want it,' he muttered as he kissed my face.

I began to fight and he pushed me against the door. I kneed him straight in the balls and ran inside to the front room where Mike and Lena were sitting. At the same time, Jase walked through the door and I was actually relieved to see him.

'Jase I need…' but before I got a chance to say any more words, Dave flipped his shit.

'This little bitch needs to go now. She tried to crack on to me and when I pushed her off, she ranted and raved about telling the police about the kids.'

'That's a lie, I did not! He is the one that cracked onto me!'

Yelling and screaming over the top of each other, I swear Jase's eyes were about to explode. He came at me and I knew I had lost the battle.

At that exact same moment, two figures outside approached the front door. Cops? Not one of us stayed to find out. We all legged it out through the back door.

I followed Mike and Lena. There was absolutely no way I wanted to be anywhere near the other two psycho's. We stopped at the car park near the oval. It was really cold and dark outside. Mike pointed to the charity clothes bin, gesturing for him and Lena to hide inside it. It looked big enough to fit all three of us. We were pretty small.

I followed them, but Mike turned around and blurted out at me, 'no not you, you're not coming. We've probably lost that squat now and it's all your fault!'

'Why do you have to cause trouble?' Lena asked me. 'Jase told me you wanted me to get caught.'

'But that's not true, I did…'

'Just get stuffed Ange!' Mike cut me off as he helped Lena inside the clothes bin. He then followed her and shut the lid behind them.

What was the point of me fighting them? They would never believe me. Not over Jase and Dave. Why did they hate me? What did I do so wrong? Asking those questions was pointless. I had to find somewhere safe for me. I had nowhere else to go.

That empty feeling came over my body again, as my sunken chest began to ache and I could feel the tears welling inside my head as the lump in my throat began to grow. I searched around for something close by, some shelter, something to hide behind. I pulled out the garbage bins that sat by the concreted wall and created a space for me to sit in. I squeezed in real tight so that no one could see me and piled some boxes up to stop the wind from reaching me.

I didn't really know what hopelessness felt like anymore. I just had this constant unsettled sinking feeling of never knowing how long a roof over my head would last for or how long I would be safe. Rule number five; never sleep on the streets at any cost. But what was I suppose to do?

Dave didn't want to be my friend, he was only nice to me cause he wanted to shag me. I realised that you don't get something for nothing. Safety in numbers rang through my head all the time. You will find safety as long as you were in a group, you were protected, you would be fine, but what if that group turned on you? And what did you have to do, or give up to be able to stay in that group? Should I have tried to get them to forgive me? Should I have let Dave have his way with me? Questions I didn't have answers to. I just didn't know what to do. I missed Daisy.

I fell into an unsettled sleep and woke up to a beeping van. As my eyes slowly opened, I was so thankful I made it through the night. I was still safe. But as soon as the van came into focus, my thankfulness turned to dread. I realised the men from the van were about to empty the clothes bin. I hoped that Lena and Mike had woken up hours ago and had already climbed out. If they got busted in there, then the cops would take them away for sure.

I held my breath as they unlocked the door and as they opened the tin box, plastic bags came rolling out along with two lifeless young bodies.

CHAPTER TEN

THE SHELTER

'Jesus Christ!' The chubby one yelled. 'Call an ambulance!'

The older man ran back to the van searching for his phone. As he dialed the emergency line and explained what had happened, the chubby man checked for any signs of life. Like true pro's, they doubled teamed giving them both CPR, pressing down on their tiny little chests. As I watched on I knew it was hopeless, I'd seen death before. I began to question if it was me? Perhaps I was jinxed. Perhaps they were right about me. I am evil. I am a bad luck charm. No one should be around me and I'm not surprised no one wanted to be around me.

For some reason I didn't cry. I stood there stuck, frozen in time, watching the scene as though I was not in my body. I could hear the distant sound of sirens coming closer and closer. Soon there would be police cars, ambulances and people drawing near. I kept my distance and backed myself up against the bins. As a streetie, it's not hard to disappear into a crowd when no one notices you anyway. I think all streeties felt that way.

The paramedics looked at each other and shook their heads like they do on TV when somebody is dead. The police held people back as they roped off the scene and began to put the two little bodies in bags. It was then that I noticed beyond the clothes bin, standing motionless, lifeless, soulless, Jase, his eyes filled with sorrow, anger and despair.

I don't know if he saw me but could not move, or if he let me run as to torment me before he took my life away. He would never forgive me for this. It was all my fault. If I let Shaggy Dave do what he wanted to do, then none of this would have happened. Why did they let me live? Why did they not let me in the clothes bin with them? Then I would have suffocated and ended this life. I didn't deserve to live. I hated myself and I hated my life. God, why didn't I die in the field that night! Why did you let me wake up! My body screamed it. Every single one of my cells exploded with the thought, why aren't I dead!

I found myself standing across the road from a youth homeless shelter on Crown Street. I stood there for what seemed like days. Blurred, lost, knowing that if I entered that building, they would send me home. I could not face home again. I didn't want to go back to that torture, but with the way things were, I was slowing dying a little more each day.

I begged from within for someone to tell me what to do.

'Hey, you wanna come in with me?'

I turned around to see a girl, about seventeen or eighteen with dreaded hair like mine. Her dreads were more defined and pink, while mine were more like a matted mess. I liked hers more.

'Um, I…' I didn't know what to say.

'Come on, it's cool. You get a three night stay, just don't tell them your real name.'

She grabbed my hand and led me across the road.

'I'm Lucy,' she said.

'I'm Ange.'

'No you're not, you're Lisa. You're sixteen, you're from Brisbane and you came to live with your cousin in Sydney because your Mum is out of the country and your Dad is dead, but she's not home, so you just want to make sure you have a bed for the night.' Lucy smirked, pretty chuffed with her elaborate lie.

'But won't they ask for ID?' I asked.

Lucy stopped just before we entered the gates and turned around to ask, 'do you even have ID?'

'No.' I replied.

'Well then what's to worry about? There was a major fire that burnt all your stuff, so you don't have a birth certificate or anything else.' She held my shoulders and looked me in the eye, 'do you want a place to stay or not?'

I nodded yes.

'Well then, let's go,' she instructed with a smile.

As we walked along the path from the front gate to the front door, I noticed a guy staring at me. I hated people staring at me but he didn't seem creepy at all. He was taller than me and built strong. Not big like huge muscles or anything, but strong. He looked as though he was the leader of the pack, surrounded by five other guys. It was like he held a silent command of their attention, their respect and he was looking directly at me.

Lucy noticed him staring at me too.

'That's Ty. If you need any glass, that's your man.' She then clicked her fingers and winked her eye.

Glass? I didn't understand.

As we arrived at the front door, Lucy swung it open revealing a brownish pathway of lino that led to an office partitioned by thick glass, with two pierced holes to talk through and an open tray to pass things through. A heavy door was bolted shut to the right of the glass wall. Made me think, what's behind there? Money? What's with the security?

From the other side, a bald short man looked up at us.

'Hi Pete.' Lucy said to the guy behind the glass. She acted like they were old friends. 'This is Lisa, she is my cousin from Brisbane.'

I wondered what had happened to my cousin not being at home and the fire and all of that?

Lucy turned around and gave me a wink, then continued, 'I kind of told her she could stay with me, but that's before I got kicked out and wound up in here and you know the story. I'll have somewhere new in a couple of days, so she can stay with me right?'

The man behind the glass stood up with papers in hand, peering over his glasses. 'Now you know the rules Lucy, you can't have guests but you do have two more nights left. Why don't we call her mother to come and get her.'

I blurted out, 'my mother is overseas and my dad is dead. I'm sixteen and want to live with Lu... Lucy.' Oops I stumbled on my words.

'Well...' he lingered, waiting for me to say my name.

'Lisa.' I said.

'Lisa? Bullsworth too?'

'No, I'm, I'm Pennyworth.' Where the hell did that come from? For some reason every time I saw a five-cent piece or even a ten-cent piece on the ground, I would pick it up and say to myself, see a penny pick it up and all day long you'll have good luck. Where did I even get that from? It certainly didn't give me any luck at all.

'Pennyworth?' He looked at me with disbelief.

'Yep, our mums are sisters.' Where did that come from as well? I was pretty good at this lying thing. I was on a role.

'Yeah, that's why we're fucked up,' Lucy snorted.

I thought he must have bought it, cause he passed through the window a clipboard with some paper and told me to fill it out. I guess Lucy's mum was pretty bad and he knew it too.

Lucy ruffled my hair with her hand and said, 'don't worry, my mum's in jail. He can't contact her anyway. Here I'll fill that out.' Then she took the clipboard and filled it out for me.

It was kinda weird. She was sort of like a punk rock guardian angel. She had her nose pierced and wore big black boots. Her smile reminded me a little of Daisy. Nowhere near as warming or trusting, but still kind and smirky, like she had it all figured out. I had no idea why she would help me, but I was grateful that she did.

'OK Lisa, rules are, no one in the rooms during the day, no drinking, smoking or taking drugs. If there are any disturbances the police will be called, no violence, no running, no aggression in the common area, rooms or halls. No outside people, no taking others into your room, stick to the female floor, no going to the male floor period...'

That word period. Ewh. At school we called it Penny or Penelope. Penelope was coming to visit and Penny had just been. I was pretty young when I got mine, eleven. I hadn't had to worry about it since being on the streets, it just never came... well actually it came once, but I don't want to talk about that.

'So you got that?' The bald man asked.

'Helllllooooo earth to Lisa?' Lucy waved her hands in front of my face.

I nodded my head. I was in. Safe. I didn't have to worry about where I would stay for the next three nights.

CHAPTER ELEVEN

LISA PENNYWORTH

It was sunny that day at the shelter. Streams of sunlight filled the center of the courtyard. There was a gate made of steel bars shielding the entrance. I wondered if it was to protect us, or them? Keep the outside world out or us streeties in? I sat down on the edge of the concreted gutter, watching people through the bars as they passed by. I don't think anyone even noticed me. Sometimes it felt like I didn't exist at all.

'You really are a daydreamer,' Lucy said, as she plonked herself down next to me.

I wondered what she wanted from me? It seemed like everyone wanted something. Nothing was done for me for free. It all came with a price. Always did. The niceness, the places to stay... something bad always happened. I was invisible to everyone else and I was used to that, but Lucy and that Ty guy, they saw me. Why?

You know it's normal for us streeties to be treated like we don't exist, we're used to it. People look right through us as though we aren't really there.

Sometimes you'll get this sneaky glance from behind the sunglasses, followed by a look of disgust as though we have rabies or something. You think we don't see it, but we do. We feel it.

'Earth to Lisa,' Lucy interrupted again.

'My name's Ange.'

'Well for the sake of the next three days, it's Lisa. I like Lisa, it suits you.'

Lucy began rolling a cigarette.

'I thought they said no smoking?' I hated smoking.

'Nah out here is fine. He meant just inside that joint,' Lucy said, pointing her chin up toward the shelter.

She lit her cigarette and began to blow smoke rings through the air. I watched a puff of smoke drift through the air as though it could exist forever, only for it to disappear. As my eyes came back into focus I could see Ty on the other side of the secured bars. He was surrounded by more streeties, again commanding their attention. He seemed so in charge.

'Come on,' Lucy said as she grabbed my arm and walked us over toward Ty.

'Hey Ty,' Lucy called out, 'this is Lisa.'

'It's Ange.'

'Yeah, yeah, whatever,' Lucy said taking a massive drag from her cigarette. 'Anything going round here? Or you down by the bridge?'

'The bridge,' he replied, pushing his dark hair back to reveal cat like green eyes. He wore a blue and white bandana wrapped around his right wrist. I think it was covering a tattoo, a name I think. I couldn't quite see it. He then added, 'one of the old corner blocks has a vacant flat. Gas is out, but you should head there, it's safe. Tia and Paul are already up there.'

Ty seemed kind. I don't know why I felt that way, I guess his eyes just seemed like he actually cared. There was no hidden agenda. He reminded me of this kid in my neighbourhood who used to look after the young ones, make sure no one harmed them.

'How may nights you got left?' he asked.

'I've got two, she just arrived today.'

'Cops been doing almost daily rounds in this joint. Lisa...' he paused, looking straight at me. 'You look too young to be here.'

'Yeah, they'd probably haul your arse out of here,' Lucy agreed.

One of the guys from inside the shelter came out and approached Ty. They slapped hands, shook, then bumped fists. It looked kinda cool. Ty nodded at Lucy and walked down the laneway, glancing my way one last time.

'Do you think they'd let me have a shower?' I asked Lucy. I couldn't quite remember the last one I had.

'Sure, go ask for the key. I'll meet you back here.'

And with that Lucy ran off down the laneway. I wondered if that was it, if I would ever see her again? She owed me nothing. She didn't have to help me.

I went back inside the building and asked the stumpy bald man for a shower. He handed me a key, told me I had five minutes otherwise they would come in and get me, in case I was planning on doing drugs in there. Apparently someone overdosed last week. I assured him that I didn't do drugs, but he looked at me like I was a liar.

The bathroom was small and really cold. It looked like a public toilet block with aluminium steel type of stuff that was cold and worn. The window was made of slides of glass and almost half of them were broken or missing. I wondered if anyone could see in. I turned on the tap and freezing cold water trickled out. I then turned on the hot tap and it turned into a trickle of boiling hot water. I spent the next two minutes trying to get the right balance and finally gave up, after all I didn't want him coming in and pulling me out.

I was glad to have washed away some of the dirt but to be honest, I still stunk. My clothes were dirty and really needed a wash. I would have to go to one of those clothes bins and grab something new. New for me but old, you know what I mean; at least they'd be clean.

My heart sank into my chest as I thought about Lena and Mike in that clothes bin. How their tiny bodies rolled out motionless, lifeless. I wondered if Jase was OK? His sister had just died. Was he looking for me? If he found me, he'd kill me. A little part of me wished that he did.

BANG BANG BANG! 'Hey Lisa it's time!' Stumpy man shouted out at me as his fist pounded on the door.

'Yep I'm out, coming!' I called back.

I threw on my clothes as quick as I could, not giving another thought to Jase. I opened the door and stumpy guy was standing right there with the phone up against his ear. He kind of pushed me toward a room with a chair.

'Wait here,' he said, 'OK?'

'Wait for what?' I asked.

'It's routine.'

'Routine what?'

He turned and walked toward the front desk, toward a woman and a police officer. I did not blink, I did not think, I did not do a second take. I knew I had to run. Lisa Pennyworth had to run. I fled down the hall, away from the desk and straight through a door into a kitchen. I stopped, panicking, circling the room. How would I get out? The windows were barred just like the front gate. Then I noticed a door! It was bolted, but not locked. I opened it and legged it across the courtyard. I jumped the fence and headed straight for the laneway and then BANG! I ran straight into Lucy. I grabbed her hand, 'cops run!' I screamed. And to my surprise she tightened her grip and said, 'this way!'

We ran.

CHAPTER TWELVE

SAFE HAVEN

Something for nothing, it does not exist. I did wonder why Lucy wanted to help me. Turns out she had a drug problem. Well she'd say, 'a healthy nibble of the goods' and I would say a massive addiction to the stuff. But that's her business. I'm no judge. How could I judge anyone in a situation like this? I had to take what I could get and this was it.

We shared an abandoned apartment with two others. Concrete floors, freezing cold with no water and no working toilet which was really annoying, especially at night. During the day it was cool cause I knew where the library was and the train station wasn't too far either. There was a cinema and a massive shopping center that had about fifty different toilets. I even knew where the fancy ones were. It would take about half an hour to walk there, so when I'd go, I'd stay for the whole day.

I finally got a whole heap of new clothes to wear. I fished them out of a Vinnie's clothes bin. The first time I did a bin run, I couldn't swallow. My neck numbed up and my arms tingled. I choked back all the welling tears into the bottom of my throat and told myself to harden the F*#@ up! I had to get new clothes. Well old for someone else, but new for me. The past had to stay the past. I couldn't think of it no more.

I got pretty tired of stinking so bad. Keeping un-smelly was really hard without water in the flat. I couldn't go back to another shelter or day center. At a day center you could get some food and have a shower, even wash your clothes if you wanted too, but until I turned sixteen it just wasn't worth the risk. So with some of the cash I got from dealing (the catch for getting help from Lucy), I'd catch a bus down to Bondi Beach and right by the ocean there was a cream building thing they called the Pavilion. It had showers and toilets. They were pretty cruddy and super cold, but the basins on the bottom of the shower were thick so I could wash my clothes and me at the same time. Lucy called it, 'two birds, one stone.' Dumb saying really. Why would you kill a bird? And how with only one stone? Anyway, I'd step on my clothes and squeeze them between my toes. People would stare at me, some would point and laugh. I didn't see what was so funny... pretty shitty actually. This one time a couple of girls pushed me around. Good thing I'd learnt to always carry a glass bottle. You can smash it real fast and either freak em out by slashing yourself or scream really loud and wave it around in the air. People will think you are crazy and then they won't mess with you. They'll run. If you play the part, they'll believe anything. I mean, if I had to, I'd glass you, but only if you attacked me first. Lucy actually gave me the idea of the glass bottle. It meant no more having to look around for a weapon if shit hit the fan, you already had that sorted if anything was to happen.

The dealing thing was getting me down. I didn't want to do it. I didn't want to take it. It scared me, but I kinda wanted to know what it was like. What it felt like? Lucy looked so peaceful and blissed out, until she came down and needed more. I once saw her OD and that scared the shit out of me. Last week she tried to bash me for some cash to buy her next hit. I figured it out pretty quickly that she wasn't going to protect me. Lucky Ty walked through the door and pulled her off me, then gave her some to tie her over until the next day. Lucy was a loose cannon, but she was all I had.

I came up with a plan to sell enough glass to stay in one of those hostel places. There were plenty of people with massive backpacks on their backs walking in and out of the ones along the main street in Kings Cross. I could do that. Shower, bed, the doors locked at night. I could put my life on my back and just cruise from hostel to hostel, not worrying about whether the cops were going to charge in, find out who I was and send me back home to a living hell, or worse, seeing Jase again! I'd sometimes get my-

self into a panic, wondering if I would see him, imaging him wrapping his hands around my neck and
squeezing hard, until every last inch of breath left my
lungs and I was dead. I hadn't told anyone about him.
Everyone knew me as Lisa and that's how it was going to stay. Even Lucy still called me Lisa.

I carried that panic with me everyday, ever since I
saw him; saw Jase. I was on the wrong side of town.
Dealers have areas and I was far out of mine. That
will never happen again! He didn't see me and after
that, I never went west. Ever.

Every Tuesday night Ty would come round to the
flat. He'd give Lucy the deal, then leave. She would
then hand out our portion to sell and then she'd get
high. For six months I had not said a word, just sat
in the corner of the room, watching it all unfold.
Ty never really looked at me. It was almost as if he
was deliberately trying not too, like I pained him or
something.

I wanted out of the flat and off the streets. I wanted
my hostel dream. I wanted to sell more glass. It's the
only way I could see me getting off the streets. So on
this particular Tuesday night I decided it was time to
talk to Ty. Something had to change.

'I'm leaving,' Ty said to Lucy as he handed her
the package. 'This is Ash your new contact.'

Ash had a thick neck and curly hair at the bottom of
his shaved head. He looked mean and didn't smile, in

fact he didn't even say hello. He looked right through me and it sent shivers down my spine. I didn't trust him at all. Ty was powerful and everyone was scared of him, including me, but I still didn't want him to go. There was kindness in his fear.

Lucy said nothing. She took the gear and then disappeared to the corner of the room, prepping for her hit. Ash walked out first and I approached Ty from behind and pulled on his arm. He didn't flinch, he just turned around and stood staring at me.

'Um, I want to do a big deal,' I said kind of trembling.

'No,' he replied and turned to walk away.

I grabbed his arm and pulled it again.

'Please, I want to get out of here. I want to do bigger deals.'

'Bigger deals?' He looked at me inquisitively.

It all clicked in my head and I realised he didn't know I was doing any deals at all. He walked toward Lucy and hit the gear out of her hand.

'Heeyyy, wha. .' Lucy said half stoned.

'Don't give the kid drugs. Not to use, not to sell.' He was serious. He was scary. He meant business.

'Oww ow ow. .' he was twisting her arm, 'OK, OK! I won't. Let me go,' Lucy pleaded.

Ty threw down Lucy's arm and walked out the door. He didn't glance back at me.

Why would he care what happened to me? It was my choice and he was ruining my dream of getting out of there. I was stuck with Lucy and the tiny pissy glass shit with no way out. I banged my head against the wall and slid down it to the floor.

Lucy laughed at me. 'You wanna do a bigger deal? There's other dealeerish...' she started her blissful state, a smile spreading across her face. 'Boys down on the grass by the overpass... big drop, them.' Her head started to slump against the wall. She managed to say two more words, 'easy, pee... shchee,' then she was out, trailed off into her drug induced state.

I moved the gear into the safe spot behind a brick on the floor and moved her so that she was lying flat on the floor and lifted her head up onto a pillow. I placed the piece of hair that was draped across her face behind her ear and thought to myself, maybe I will get my wish after all... a bag on my back, a new life to live.

CHAPTER THIRTEEN

TY

I remember that day. I remember it all too clearly. It's ingrained in my memory no matter how hard or what I have done to forget it; it's never gone away. I woke up that morning with a distinct husk in my throat. It felt like a swollen lump, like a piece of bread that just won't go down.

'You right Ange?' Lucy asked me while brushing her teeth.

I nodded yes, when really I meant no.

'You want to back out of this thing? It's going to be easy you know. We're grabbing the gear, dropping it off to someone else, that's it! Easy peasy.' She smiled at me through the moulded mirror hanging on the bathroom wall. 'Ha!' she exclaimed, 'we're modern day drug mules! No selling, no buying, just carrying from seller to buyer. The dealer is the one that takes all of the risk you know Lisa,' she said shaking her toothbrush at me.

I trailed off. It was one of Lucy's really long rants, about how she knows what's really going on in the world. She once went on and on about the corrupt police, about how they are the ones leading the drug trade and busting the ones that aren't in the know, cause they still have to look like they're doing their job.

'So, we just gotta stay with this dealer, this dude in Kings Cross. He's in with the cops.'

I just nodded and agreed. What did I know anyway?

'… And in Columbia, well…' Lucy stopped and clicked her fingers in front of my face, 'are you listening?'

'Yeah, have you got some Panadol?' I asked.

'Panadol!' Lucy burst out laughing, slapping her knee like it was the funniest thing she'd ever heard.

'Honey, we got everything but Panadol! You'll be right.' And with that she slapped me on the back and walked out of the bathroom.

I stood leaning against the basin, staring at myself in the mirror. Something didn't feel right. I wanted to splash some water on my face and wash the sickened doubt I felt down the drain, but Lucy just used the last of the water we bottled yesterday, brushing her teeth.

We headed to the wrong side of our town, Woolloomooloo. Just a hop skip and a jump from Kings Cross, in fact they are basically next door to each other. How could it be the wrong side? Like the west side of New York, or is it the east side or the west side of America? Well whatever they meant by the wrong side over there, this was it. Who'd have thought you could get much wronger than KX. I could feel it turning in my tummy, making me feel sick. I started rubbing my belly like it was a washing machine going round and round.

'Knock it off Lisa. What ya so nervous for?'

I didn't answer Lucy, I knew she was nervous too. I was just grateful she didn't have a hit before we left. She did stupid shit and said stupid shit every time she was high. I always tried to convince her to stay inside after she got trashed otherwise there'd be a fight, then she would get arrested and we'd all be busted, cause when you're on that shit, you just can't help but tell the truth and get yourself and every other bloody person that's in your life into trouble AND that included me! So it was always safer indoors than out. I was nervous.

As we walked toward the meeting point, down the long back street that connected KX to Wools, I caught a glimpse of myself in a window. Scrawny me. My hair almost fully dreaded, the blonde blackened by dirt and lack of care. When I last washed it, I had no idea. My clothes hung on me like wet blankets on a line, limp and lifeless. My skin pale, much paler than it had been before. Eating left overs, stale food thrown out, cheap McDonald's or a pie, well it will do that to you. I would hardly ever drink. I loved coke! You know it's cheaper than water. My schoolteacher used to say, 'it'll rot your teeth.' I was lucky that hadn't happened yet. Not sure what I'd do if they did. Not like I could afford a dentist.

I know it seems stupid but I missed clean hair, and I missed fresh sheets too. Actually I missed sheets all together. I didn't have any. Well I did have some at one point, but you know what it's like, people in and out of that place, they go missing, everything does. I missed clean fresh smelling clothes and dresses too. I never thought I'd say that! A dress! Seriously, I used to hate them. Getting ready for church on a Sunday morning at 9am. My hair would be brushed and pulled back, my face washed and wiped, then a dress pulled on over the top of my head, something pink and frilly, YUCK. Well yuck was what I used to think way, way, way before my Dad left, before my mum starting drinking and before my step dad arrived. My mum used to say that Dad left because he hated me, because I was a pain in the arse. I remember how she used to spit and foam at the mouth telling me how bad I was, how stupid I was, how she couldn't stand me. What a slut I was. I never even knew what that word meant. I still don't really... but that was a long time ago now.

Sometimes I'd find myself staring at other girls, watching them laugh and smile, flipping their shinny hair over their shoulders, revealing a fun bright coloured strap, leading to a handbag full of money. Nice clean shoes, some with a small heel, almost gliding across the pavement. Their dresses all kinds of different colours, swishing in the breeze. I wanted to be like them... but that was far from the girl I saw in the reflection of the window.

'Jesus Lisa,' Lucy grabbed me by the arm. 'You're friggin off in la la land all the bloody time!'

I struggled to keep up with her, almost jogging down the street. I didn't know why she was in such a hurry. Maybe she took something after all.

We arrived at the spot of the pick up. Lucy pulled out a key she was given three days ago. She was told what to do and what lock the key would fit. Inside the restaurant back door, we would find a locked cupboard containing a backpack full of the goods. I guess it was kind of smart. The dudes in control would plant the drugs while casually eating their lunch. No one else would be aware.

So we walked in through the back door. No one blinked an eye as Lucy unlocked the bottom draw below the sink and took out a backpack that was stuffed inside. Lucy was told to leave the key in the lock, signaling that we had taken it. So we did just that.

'OK, step two,' she said, 'we gotta make the drop. When we give them the backpack, they will give us a bill, like a takeaway bill, which I'll give back to the dude in control and then we'll get paid. Just like that! Cool huh! No looking out for cops, no wondering if we'll get jumped...'

'But what if we get jumped now?' I asked.

Lucy kind of snorted, 'nah that won't happen, no one knows we're doing the deal.' Then she stopped as though having second thoughts. It was possible we could get jumped. People knew we deal, it's just one of those things, if someone else was desperate enough (and all us streeties were desperate enough) then we could get jumped.

We left the restaurant back door, eye balling everyone as we walked. I kept repeating in my mind, act cool, act cool, wondering if people could see the terror in my face or at least see my pulsating heart coming out of my chest. It felt like it was bouncing a mile out of my skin, just like you see in cartoons.

Lucy put her hand on my shoulder so I knew she meant business. 'Now listen to me, we're coming up to Billows Lane. Two exits. One in, one out. What I want you to do is walk in with the backpack. I'll go round the other side of the laneway and make sure the coast is clear. If I call out, um, um…' she looked around for a word, 'yellow pop, then the exit is blocked, OK? Then ya gotta run. We both do.'

As if reading my mind, wanting to back out, Lucy continued, 'it's going to be OK. Only one dude is meeting us on this side. When we come round the corner, I'll make sure there is just the one, then as you walk up to him, I'll check out the other side, make sure we both get out. OK?'

She didn't wait for my reply and said, 'OK. Good. Let's go.'

I can't really remember why I didn't insist on being the one to go around the back. I guess Lucy seemed like she was doing the more dangerous part, going round the back, after all the entrance was wide and fairly busy. If you were coming up the back way, well, you could get jumped more easily.

As we approached the laneway we could see only one guy standing on the corner. He had his back to us, but he didn't look so big. Maybe he was a bit taller than me, but probably just as scrawny. That meant he was probably a junkie with not much strength at all.

'OK, I'll run round the back, remember yellow pop,' Lucy called out as she ran off.

As I approached the guy standing by the entrance, the feeling in my stomach started to tighten. Everything inside me told me to run so I started to reason with it. But why should I run? And what would Lucy say? What would happen if we didn't give this guy the backpack? And what about the bill thing we had to pick up and pass on? What would the dude in charge do to us? My mind began to spiral out of control, convincing me it was better to step forward and pull on his jumper, then it was to run.

As I put my hand out, he turned around, slowly blowing smoke out from his mouth. For me it was like slow motion, being frozen in time. Step by step each feature being revealed, as though I was putting together a puzzle description of someone I used to know. But it didn't take long for me to work out who this guy was, I knew it as soon as the smoke ring opened up across my face; it was Jase.

The first blow came quick and I dropped to my knees, my head hitting the concrete. He dragged me by the backpack deep into the laneway. My left ear buried, immersed in a shallow pool of water. I couldn't hear anything out of my right ear. I had been deaf in that ear since that night in the field, since I ran away from that hellhole. I guess that is why I didn't hear Lucy scream, 'YELLOW POP, YELLOW POP!' I had no idea how many of his crew were coming up that laneway. What I remember was Jase saying, 'this bitch killed my sister!' as he ripped off the backpack.

I screamed and kicked as they held me down, a sharp stab in my arm as they injected me with that poison. I started to lose consciousness as they ripped of my pants. I could taste the blood that was running down from my nose. I chose to focus on that instead of the brutality that was occurring. I could see Jase's red shoes, a bright red leather, massive in size, white thick soles with a small hint of my blood and black washed tips from stepping in the puddle by my head. They were new... the shoes were new.

My eyes began to roll into the back of my head when I heard the explosion, BANG, BANG! It was gunshots. At first I thought it was at me, that he had finally killed me, ending my suffering after the most horrific suffering a girl could feel. I heard feet running, scurrying off as fast as they could. As I blinked

and moved my head an inch to the side, I saw him…
it was Ty.

Gun in hand he bent down and lifted me up with
no effort at all. I felt his footsteps running and Lucy's
voice. I then closed my eyes for what I hoped was for
good. God take me now. I do not want to wake.

But I did wake. Curled up in a car. I was lying on
the front passenger seat. It was lowered as far back
as it would go. Ty was driving, enraged. I blinked a
few times as if to say, 'am I alive?' It was almost as
though he heard my thoughts and Ty turned and said
to me, 'you're going to be OK.'

Maybe I would. Maybe I would live, but my soul
had died. It was gone for good.

'Why? Why did you…?' I trailed off, unable to
finish my sentence.

He looked down at his wrist and then out of the
window, as though he was facing a fact that there was
someone else once that he could not save.

I had noticed before, in a fight between Ty and
this meathead, the bandana wrapped around his forearm was covering a tattoo. R.I.P. Chloe was engraved
on his wrist and above it a golden haired mural of a
young girl. Ty had been strong and grabbed this meathead by the throat. The meathead had tried to claw his
way out, ripping the bandana away.

Weary and tired, I closed my eyes, vowing I would
never cry again. How can you cry when your soul has

been taken from you? Where do the tears come from
if your soul is dead?

CHAPTER FOURTEEN

MELBOURNE

My mother used to say to me, be careful what you wish for. It's the one time she was right. I should never have wished for a bag on my back and a new life to live, because I got it. I got a massive bag of shit on my back, lugging it around every day and every night. And just like all the other old backpacks, I stored it; I buried it in the back. But instead of a cupboard I chose to bury it deep within my soul... the soul that withered and died that day in the car.

It was a long trip to Melbourne, well not for me, but for Ty. Me passed out, half dead, in a drug induced state. Ty in a rage, hating himself for not being able to save me before it was too late. He had seen so many girls go down that way and he didn't want that for me.

We never left Melbourne. Ty saw it as an opportunity for the both of us. He silently vowed to always keep me safe, keep me away from the streets... and that he did. I didn't go anywhere near the streets, not for six whole years. He got us a house out in Caulfield.

It was pretty old inside, but all the windows had glass and curtains too!

I didn't go back to school because of the whole identification thing. I didn't want anyone to know who I was and that was OK with Ty. He never pressured me nor made me feel bad, instead he paid for someone else to come round and teach me to read. I mean, I could already read, kind of, but they helped me read some more. Ty taught me to type and to use a computer too. He told me the Internet would be big and that I needed to learn it. I had no idea what that was or what it meant at the time. Besides that one guy who helped me to read, no one else ever came to the house, not one single person. I didn't mind.

Ty had two ways of getting to work. One was a rusted old car that he left at the station three suburbs over and the other was a motorbike he kept in the shed out back. He said, that way no one would know where we lived and that I would always be safe.

He didn't tell me who he was working for, but I knew the guy. I had met him once and once only. It was the first night we drove into Melbourne. Tired, ruined, almost destroyed, I was lying down in the car. I managed to sit up and noticed a brightly lit warehouse, which really wasn't big at all. I pushed off the woolen blanket that Ty had placed on top of me and stared straight out the window. There was an Asian man, taller than Ty, his arms thick with muscles, commanding full attention from the circle of men. He looked more powerful than Ty and I wondered how that could possibly be.

Ty regularly threw out his phone. They were on a constant rotation. A new phone then three months would go by and it would hit the bin. He'd get a new phone, then another three months go by, bin. This one time Ty thought he had lost his phone, only I had pulled it out from his jacket. I read through the text messages and I knew it was no good. I didn't know what he was moving and shipping, but it was pretty dangerous stuff. He didn't want me to know because he wanted me out of danger and far away from the guys he knew in the underworld.

What he was involved in was far more serious, far more dangerous than anything I had seen in KX. It wasn't drugs. He would never deal in that market again. I don't know if it's because of what happened to me or if he always felt guilty dealing drugs. He didn't take it, he didn't touch it; he did what he had to do.

I don't know if you have ever noticed but the successful ones never dabble in the goods. They don't fry their brains. They are smarter than the rest.

Ty was brilliant. He was more than just my saviour, he was my protector too. He would bring me books so that I could read and movies to watch. He really wanted me to do a course and get a normal job, but first he was going to do one last deal. He said he wanted out and that once this last deal was done, we would move north, start a fresh new life with new identities.

I never had an identity. I threw it out that day in the field. I didn't want to be Angela Browski damaged goods. But I also didn't want to be Ange, nearly dead goods. Or stupid arse Lisa Pennyworth, who had no luck at all dealing glass. Now I was simply A, that's what Ty called me. I was living a simplistic life reading books. I wanted to help other girls like me, the ones on the streets. Stop them from getting to where I got. Find them and help them. I didn't know how, but I knew I had to do something.

I remember when child protection services came to my house. It was just four years before I ran away from that evil home. My mum threatened me and I was scared. I was a child that should never have been put in a position that had to make those kinds of decisions. I was manipulated by hope for the better, that the house would be different and in fear of her words, "I will kill you. You will never see the light of day." Ha! In retrospect that would have been so much better than the nightmare my life became. Anyway, child protection services left, as they always did and then the mental and emotional abuse got worse, scarring me forever. It became unbearable. It's funny how people don't know and don't realise, but I was told to pack my bags and leave almost every single day. Where was I supposed to go? Here I guess, the streets, where I ended up.

I never told Ty any of this nor did I tell him what I wanted to do for other girls like me. I knew that he wouldn't laugh, but I just didn't want to talk about it. I knew that if I approached the subject of helping other girls, it would go hand in hand with talking about my past. Then the why's and the how's would bring back flooding memories, tearing down years of walls that I had built up. Those walls were barely keeping me sane. I wasn't ready for those walls to come down yet. No, I didn't want to talk about the past. I wasn't ready for that. Don't get me wrong, I was strong, stronger than I had ever been. Ty made sure of that.

Ty hung a punching bag up inside the shed. We would spend hours in there, sparring, kicking the shit out of that bag. It was like all the anger welled up inside of me would go straight through the leather and into a locked room in the center of that bag. Some days I would think about lighting it up and watching it burn, letting it smoulder on the concrete floor, soaked with my tears and the blood that I've tasted, the violations that have occurred. I buried all of it, fists full of it, deep into that bag.

Then one day, just like every other day, I went out to the shed. I put on my gloves and began the blows, penetrating the bag as hard as I could.

I didn't hear the shed door open; I was too zoned into the bag. I did however feel a brush of wind touch the back of my neck, as the hairs stood on end. As fast as a flash, I dropped to a squat, then twisted back up.

I came back up with a right hook, but with pure ingenious craft, Ty blocked me and sent me down to the ground.

'Jesus Ty!'

He had shot me down in one fell swoop, his hand flat against my chest, keeping me pinned to the floor.

'OK, OK!' I boxed his arm away.

'Was that necessary?' I asked, grimaced with annoyance rather than pain. And with that he grabbed my arm and twisted it round my back.

'And what if this wasn't me A, what would you do now?'

With a flexible back kick, I struck his kidney and rolled myself out of the hold that he had.

Ty held out his hand and helped me back up onto my feet. 'Good,' he said.

Without grabbing his gloves he began to box the bag much harder than you normally would if you were punching with bare hands.

'You've been gone longer than normal,' I said. 'It's been five days. Is everything OK?' I asked. 'Where have you been?'

Ty stopped and looked at me for a second before continuing to punch the bag.

'You don't have to worry A.'

'I know but...'

'Everything's OK.'

He didn't look at me, he just kept boxing the bag. I turned and walked out of the garage and left him to it.

As I walked down by the side of the shed and toward the side gate, I could hear the deep grunts of anxious thought slamming into that bag. Somehow by the sound of the grunts I knew everything was not OK. Then, when I turned the corner and saw that he went against all of the rules that he had sternly put in place, I knew for sure it wasn't going to be OK. He came back with a truck and it was sitting in our driveway.

CHAPTER FIFTEEN

JAIL

I must have read the same page three times. It was useless. I threw the book down to the floor and sunk back into my bed. I cupped my face with my hands and allowed myself to indulge in stupid thoughts of police banging down the door and hauling us away in the back of a van.

BANG BANG! I jumped a mile.

'A?'

Oh thank god! It was Ty, knocking on my bedroom door.

'Come in,' I said.

Ty opened the door and stood half in and half out of my room. Ready for a quick escape, I thought.

'Everything is going to be OK,' he said.

'I know.' I lied.

His eyes looked worried and his knuckles were stained with blood, probably from bashing away at the bag for the last hour and a half. Still, I dared not ask, but I was worried. That was the third time he told me everything was going to be OK.

'Everything is going to be OK,' he repeated again, leaning against the frame of the door. 'I wanted to make sure everything was in place before telling you... this is the last job.'

A huge grin came over my face, could this be it forever? No more wondering when he will come home, if he will come home at all.

'Seriously?' I asked, not really believing what I had just heard.

'The lease is up next week and we are out of here.'

'But how? I mean where are we going?' I was a little confused. We had talked about going north, maybe buying a boat, cruising about. Ty loved boats. He grew up on them. Him and his sister used to have tinny races up the Murray. He said he felt safe on the water. That I would feel safe there too.

'I'll have the rest of the money in two days. We can go right up to the top, Darwin or Cairns. We'll flip a coin, grab a boat up there. You can do a course, whatever you like. I'll have your new identity ready to go.'

I couldn't believe it!

'You got it?' I asked, shocked, surprised, a cluster of feelings echoing through my voice.

'I got it. Just two more days, we'll pick it up with the money.'

I jumped off the bed and threw my arms around his neck. This was everything I wanted. A real new life, a new start, no more Angela, no more Ange, no more Lisa Pennyworth and even no more A! Even though I liked A, I'd be happy to let that go too.

'Ty! Thank you! Thank you!' I felt so much joy inside and hope revived.

'I promised you,' he almost whispered in my ear and I knew what he was referring to. After what had happened that day in Wool KX, I never wanted to sleep on the streets again and Ty swore to me that I never would.

I squeezed him even tighter.

I could see the boat, beautiful pristine white, like the colour of freshly bleached sheets. The sails lightly floating through the breeze, curling and swaying in their own style of dance. There was a wave from the deck, a gorgeous glistening smile from a perfectly built man. I ran down the wooden dock and skipped over the side of the boat, landing next to him. I embraced my saviour, this wonderful man and drew in a long gentle breath. I smelt his aroma and it filled my body with hope, joy, belief. I looked up into his eyes, seeing so many more colours than I'd ever seen before. I felt love. A sense of peace. I melted into his arms. For the first time I saw a tenderness that I wanted wrapped around my body, never letting me go. But something was wrong. The boat began to move in a way that clearly not only frightened me but Ty too, as he latched onto me with one arm, clutching the mast with the other, fear filling his eyes.

A roaring thunder bellowed and I was startled by yelling and the sound of a pole being shoved through the middle of the front door. Completely awake from my dream, I ran out of my bedroom into a room full of people screaming, 'get down on the floor! Get down on the floor now!'

I was grabbed from behind and pushed to the floor, grazing my chin on the carpet.

'Let her go! She's got nothing to do with this!' I heard Ty scream.

I tried to struggle, to get a glimpse of Ty, but it was useless. There were two officers holding me down, one with a knee in my back. A little unnecessary don't you think?

I continued to struggle and called out to Ty, as they took him away. He repeatedly screamed, 'LET HER GO!' as they dragged him away. It was then the two bodies holding me down began their speech, 'this is the Australian Federal Police, you are under arrest...' they were reading me my rights. It was then that I knew we were truly fucked.

Down at the station they grilled me for hours. I had no idea what was going on. I didn't even know what Ty had done. I guess he was clever that way, if I never knew what he had done, then they couldn't put me in jail. I was scared for him. They kept screaming the name Pho. 'You know who Pho is! Tell us who the truck was going to.'

They played good cop and bad cop, they finger printed me and put me in a cell. I didn't have any ID so they couldn't confirm who I was, which surprised me after all the places I had broken into before I went to Sydney. Not one fingerprint had ever been record-ed. Lucky me.

I was sure they would let us out soon, but morning came and there was no release. I asked to speak to Ty, to which they answered, no. Actually it was, 'you're dreaming... no!'

My cell was small with only a bench made from hard plastic. I couldn't lie down on it cause it wasn't long enough. There was blood on the wall and stains on the ground. It was disgusting. Some streeties talk about going to jail like they have won a prize. Food on the table, a warm shower, free clothes... but this all felt like death to me. Cold, hard, brutal anguish. I just wanted out. I thought perhaps that fake imaginary God people go on about so much might actually be listening to me that day. Fat chance!

Legal Aid arrived and it was then that I learned that Ty was in for dealing arms. I think that's worse than drugs. The massive big score he always talked about, the one that would get us out forever, it was selling a shipment of guns. Good money, great jail time. That meant he was facing six to eight years.

It was like someone grabbed a spoon and pierced my chest, slowly, forcefully finding all the old shit

I had buried in that hole and started to scoop it out. The memories started to flood back, preparing me for a new life back on the streets. Ha! There you go, that new life again. Wishing will get you nowhere!

My legal aid advised me to tell the police who I really was so that they could identify me and then let me go. It was obvious that I knew nothing and was not a part of it at all, plus it didn't matter if they knew my name, I was over age, I could do whatever I wanted. Being nineteen, the police could not send me home nor notify my mother of where I was, that's if she was still alive.

Ty signed a confessional statement stating that he did it all. No other involvement, not even from Pho. I was released a few hours later, released back onto the streets.

So he left me. Ty broke his promise. He took care of Pho instead of me. So I had my freedom and a new life to live… back to being Angela Browski, well you can call me Ange.

CHAPTER SIXTEEN

I DID WHAT I HAD TO DO

Ty was smart, not telling me anything. He never told me a single thing. He kept me in the dark so that I could never be arrested for what he was doing to support us, to make our dreams come true. With all that smartness you'd think there'd be a backup plan! Everything in the house was seized, the lease ended and I had no money... I did what I had to do.

I opened my eyes in yet another apartment, not a couch this time nor the floor, but in a bed next to someone I didn't even know.

'Time for you to go,' he grunted and threw my clothes at me. I'd only slept for four maybe five hours, but I survived another night, I was safe... well sort of.

I pulled my pants up and rubbed my face, not remembering much at all. A few twenties on the dresser... I did what I had to do.

The first time was the hardest. I'd never really had a positive experience in that way and didn't really

know what all the fuss was about in movies. I simply
didn't believe in love. It didn't feel good. It felt like
ants under my skin, itching, trying to get out. I held
my breath and kept forgetting to breathe out. Every
muscle in my body was tense. It felt so unnatural to
be choosing this. Normally it was taken from me, but
now I was doing the choosing. My body was stiff as
a board, fighting him off from the inside, without actually ever moving at all. I didn't cry, that doesn't
happen to me, not anymore. It's like my body, my
chest, had a disconnected wire. I guess that wire was
no longer fused to the spot where my heart used to
be. I wasn't exactly emotionless, I just didn't feel any
tears. Like someone who tries to cry but can't. You
get this weird feeling of disconnect. The pain is still
there yet it's wrapped under a wrapper and twisted
shut. I didn't feel the edges anymore but I knew it
was there. It niggled at me from time to time. In the
moment when his hand awkwardly grabbed my breast
and he forcefully entered me, I felt the wrapper scrap-
ing the hollow spot in the center of my chest, where
the wires used to connect. Then it was over. He paid
for the room and I slept. I slept until the guy at the
front desk banged repeatedly on the door and told me
it was time to leave.

When I walked out the door, I remember looking
back over my shoulder as though I was saying goodbye to someone. I'm not sure who, it's not like I'd
been a normal girl, not since way before that day in

the field. Yet when I looked back at the sheets all messed up, draped over the aging mattress, I think there was a last remaining part of her that finally disappeared. My eyes closed for a second and I breathed in, pushing the vile smell of sweat and semen away from my mind, picturing a single yellow flower, bright in colour as though it was smiling, standing still, not judging me, not badgering me, not telling me that I was a whore. Not agreeing that my mother was right to call me that when I was ten, as though she were a prophet and that this was all I was ever meant to be. Daisy I miss you, I thought to myself, I wonder where you are? I wondered if heaven existed at all.

A few months went by and I hooked up with Ty's old crew. They knew my name and were expected to protect me in Ty's honour because he kept his word and didn't bring the empire down with him. How stupid is he! To think I idolized the sucker. Those dudes had no honour. I slept with half of them for a couch to sleep on.

It wasn't too long till I was back working with packages again, only this time I wasn't dealing. I went back to Lucy's idea; the drug mule modern style. Just carrying from one spot to another.

I was trustworthy to Pho's crew because I had nowhere else to go. They kept it quiet from Ty (not like he could find out too much from inside), but he'd kill me if he knew I was hanging with Pho's crew.

It started off small like it always does, minor stuff like passing dope. Sometimes I needed to hold the gear for an hour or maybe a day, carrying it from one place and dropping it somewhere else. It was easy money and as the packages got bigger, so did my pay. Soon I was carrying rock from one big hit to another. Was it dangerous? Yeah whatever, I could hold my own. What did I really have to lose? No home, no Ty, no friends, no anything left, not even the hope of going to do a course or moving somewhere new. That dream was gone, as was Angela Browski. I should have just left her years ago. Why did I bother for those six years with Ty? Wasted time.

I wasn't running with anyone in particular nor did I have a permanent address. Once the money started to roll in, I stayed in hostels. I didn't trust anyone in squats and I avoided the streets at all costs. I could get into a dorm room pretty cheap, especially if the room was big. The more they fit in, the cheaper the bed, which was OK with me. I didn't have talk to anyone and I felt safer there.

My first night on the streets without Ty was the hardest. I went back to the house and sat by the shed, my knees curled up into my chin, wishing it was all a mistake or that Pho would come forward and get him out, or even that the police would find new evidence and they'd let him go. But deep down I knew it was a pipe dream, a dream that would never eventuate. I hated Ty so much that night for leaving me, for breaking his promise, when all he was really trying to do was protect me and give me a new life. I hadn't been to see him in jail. I thought that if he looked at me he would see emptiness, just a shell of the girl he once knew. She was gone. I didn't give myself any hope because what was the point? Just as it was all coming together for me, God swept it away again.

After Ty went inside, I stopped looking at other girls on the street and wondering how I would help them or think about how I could show them a way out... there's no way out. Why give them false hope just to tear it all away, for them to be destroyed again. I decided I might as well ignore them, just like the rest of society ignores them, ignores us, as they walk to work trying not to look at us. You treat us as though we do not exist and you wonder why we hang together and steal your bags and shit. Can't you hear us scream out? We need you! But you don't need us and that is why things will never change. There is no hope for us.

I was having one of those nights. I didn't get to run a deal. My change was out, I had no food, but I didn't care about that, I was used to going hungry. What I cared about was spending a night inside behind a closed door; a door that locked. The second night without Ty, I slept inside a slide. It was a tubular slide and I shouldn't say sleep because I was awake all night, terrified to breathe in case someone heard me. I was terrified of another Jase out there, with six other friends, way too many for me to fend off. Ty taught me to fight well and I could take on two maybe three at a time, but not a whole group (even three was pushing it). At least with the new way of getting a room, I was doing it, it was on my terms. I let you choose me. You think it would chip away at me, eat me up from the inside out, but I had already lost my soul and when you have no soul you have nothing to lose and only a safe place to sleep to gain. I was all alone, so I had to do what I had to do.

'Hey Ty,' I said down the telephone.

'Are you alright A?' he asked.

'Yeah I'm fine. I'm staying with Cassie, comfy couch, got some work again tomorrow.' I carefully breathed when I choked back the lies, as they would get caught in my throat and I didn't want Ty to think that there was something else going on.

'I'm going to be out as soon as I can. Just stay off the streets OK A? I'll try and get some money to you. I'll try and get a message to... well you know... but it's hard because of... you know.'

'It's fine Ty, don't worry, everything is alright.' I choked back more lies deep into my throat.

'The two charges of conspiracy have been dropped. I'll probably only do five years.'

I held the phone against my chest, clenching my eyes shut, partly with despair.

'Oi, you coming or what?' A man standing next to the phone booth yelled out at me.

I nodded to him, 'yes'. I had another drop the next day, but it meant I needed somewhere to sleep that night with no money. The next deal I was doing would see me safe for a couple of weeks, so it was only for that night. I was doing what I had to do.

'Ty, I gotta go. That's great news about your sentence. I'll come see you soon.'

CHAPTER SEVENTEEN

SAMMY

Another day on the job and this one was a big one. I excitedly almost skipped the whole way there. This deal alone was worth eight hundred bucks! I couldn't believe it when Jimmy told me. Ah Jimbo! You bloody legend! This meant a whole month off the streets for me. I could get a bed in a hostel for ninety bucks a week. Hold up… my maths was pretty bad. If I stole what I ate, took seconds and shit, then I could have like almost two months off the streets! Boy did my brain start ticking over. If I could do this every week, I could like buy a caravan or something!

I bent over in pain, as a twinge under my rib crippled me. 'Get your shit together Ange, stop being a pussy!' I told myself.

Yep I would talk to myself sometimes. It was the only real company I had. I'd go insane if I didn't, or maybe I'd go insane if I did? Either way I was pretty much screwed, besides I was being a pussy. I did eighty-six push-ups that morning. I was upping my training after I got jumped last week and barely made it out and it was against only one dude! Far from the training that Ty once put me through. I reckon he'd be pretty disappointed in me. Anyway, the bigger the drops I made, the more risk, so I had to make sure I could handle it.

I walked down the path across the main road and toward the underpass. I wondered why the hell they always chose the dodgiest places to meet up for this kind of shit? But then I remembered, no cops. They were never around those types of places. I was pretty careful with shit like that.

I wasn't breaking into people's houses cause the cops had my fingerprints on file. It wasn't worth the risk. I mean you wouldn't get much anyway and then you have to try and convince someone else to sell what you did steal using their ID or a fake ID because no bloody bastard in those pawn shops will take it on the dodge no more. It totally put us streeties out of business. Well not entirely, there was other stuff like jumping cars or people, but none of that sat well with me. M Double D M, I called me. Modern Day Drug Mule. Yep that was perfect for me.

I turned the corner to the underpass and almost walked straight into the kid that was picking up. I really had to get my head out of the clouds and start paying attention. It's that kind of shit that could get you jumped, not looking at your surroundings.

'Alright steady on,' said the skinny one with his pants down around his knees. He was sixteen at most.

Skinny pants down's leader, stood against the wall smoking a cigarette like he believed he invented them. You know the ones. They exhale like a train sitting on ice, puffing it out before it actually goes in. They were typical newbies trying to take on the drug world.

'You here for Pho's gear?' I asked the train puffer, as the weedy pants kid continued to stare me down. I felt like picking him up by his pants, giving him a good shake until they were back up around his waist, then tightening the belt so tight that he'd never get them off!

'You the dropper?'

'Nah I'm the stopper,' I said sarcastically and they looked at me confused.

I threw the backpack down at their feet. 'It's in the bag. Make the call and say it's been dropped.'

Train puffer pulled out his phone and turned his back to me as though to keep the privacy. What a dick. These are MY people dude!

I kicked back against the concrete wall and waited for the all-good signal so I could get out of there, grab my cash and get a place to stay.

As I leaned back against the wall, I heard a chirpy yet annoying whistling tune come from down the other end of the tunnel. We all sort of stiffened our backs and stood upright as a figure walked toward us. As the figure came into the light at our end of the tunnel, I could see that it was actually a he, an aboriginal kid, probably about twelve years old. He was short with matted hair almost as bad as mine. He gave me a grin and a cheeky little wink that made me question, who the fuck is this guy?

'Hey bro he's back,' the weedy one said to the puffer.

Without waiting for a response the weedy kid jumped the black kid, pounding his head as the kid kicked and screamed, 'let me go!'

Now I'm not one to get into a fight if I don't have to. I'll defend when I need to and walk away when it's not my fight to bear, but this kid... well he was just a small kid and younger than the both of them.

'Get off him!' I yelled.

The puffer got off his phone and said, 'deals done bitch, get out of here.'

My back and neck immediately stiffened and I could feel the adrenaline beginning to rise up my spine and pump down into my arms. I knew where all the exits were.

'Let him go.' The words left my lips coldly. No expression at all.

'Or what?' Said the smart arse weedy one.

I put my hand into my pocket as though I was about to pull out a knife and told them quite blankly, 'don't piss me off or you'll go on Pho's list. That's if I let you get away unscarred.'

It really was pathetic watching the leader try to stare me down, while his weedy shadow couldn't take his eyes off my pocket, shaking ever so slightly, wondering if it was a knife or a gun that I stored in my puffed up jacket pocket. Normally with the young newbies, you just got to bark a bit till they back off... they scare real easy. I mean, of course I also did have a knife in my pocket and I would have used it too, if I had to.

Puffy McPuff threw his cigarette away and nodded at the weedy one to get off the young boy.

'Woo hoo suckers!' The black kid chimed out, cartwheeling toward the path.

'Yeah, whatever abo, if we catch ya again...'

'You'll what?' I said.

Exactly, they would turn around and walk away, just like they did that day. Sometimes I wondered if it was me that was so scary or if it was the name Pho. More people were scared of him than I had realised. It was too late for me to become uninvolved with him, but I knew why Ty kept me a secret, kept me out of that world. Fingers and toes go missing, people too. You don't want to cross him.

'Hey, what's your name?' I called out to the kid I just saved.

'Sammy.'

He put his hand out to shake mine.

'Ange.' I replied.

When I put my hand out to shake his, he let out a 'HA!' and slicked his hair back, leaving my hand hanging in mid air. Little shit.

'You know I had them back there,' he said in a cheery and very cocky voice. 'I was just about to Kung Fu their ass. Woo HA!' he sung out, although he sounded more like a hyena than Bruce Lee, kicking and flicking his legs around.

'Sure Sammy,' I said back to him, totally unconvinced he could throw a single good punch. I actually considered drop kicking his ass to prove a point.

'What were you doing?' he asked, genuinely unsure of what had just happened.

'Never you mind,' I said, not knowing why the kid was still by my side.

I noticed we were continuing to walk in the same direction, but neither one of us asked where the other was going. There was kind of an awkward silence. It was time for me to tell the kid that it was the end of the road for us, when out of nowhere Samm said, 'knock, knock?'

I couldn't resist. 'Who's there?'

'Turnip.'

'Turnip who?'

'Turnip the volume, it's quiet in here.'

It was the lamest joke I had ever heard but I couldn't stop laughing. I don't know what it was but the more I laughed the more he laughed and soon we were bent over on the grass, giggling like five-year-old girls. I couldn't remember the last time I laughed like that. Actually I couldn't remember the last time I laughed at all. It had been three years since Ty went to jail and I think that was the first time I laughed since all that happened.

We laid on our backs, choking out our last breaths of laughter. Staring up into the sky, Samm said to me, 'look, can you see that?' And he pointed up into the clouds excitedly like he just discovered a new species. 'It's a tiger! Cool huh?'

It actually was pretty cool. The cloud had the shape of a tail, whipped like fresh cream. The body was fluffy like you could jump on it and disappear into its white center. The sun was sparkling through a hole, creating an eye.

'Look at that one,' I pointed up toward the sky, 'it looks like a house,' I said. We both stared at it and I wondered if he was imaging a warm cozy bed with fresh white sheets and some warm freshly baked bread too.

'How old are you Sammy?' I asked, rolling my head to the side, looking to see if he showed any signs of his age.

'Thirteen.' He paused for a second then rolled his head to the side to catch a glimpse of any signs of age on my face. He then asked, 'you?'

'Twenty three... I think.'

'Ha! You old school. You look like thirty-five.'

'Hey!' I said, pinching his arm.

'Yeah you look old and shit. Scary old lady gonna beat up those kids.'

'You little shit'

I chased him around the park as he teased me, playing the role of an old lady. It was probably the most fun I'd had. It reminded me of Lena and running through the park, laughing away. We were Sammy's age back then, before she suffocated in the clothes bin. Charity killing the charity cases. I had to ask myself, what if I killed this boy too? There is a reason why I didn't let anyone come close to me. Death followed me like a bad stench that just wouldn't wash off. I decided not to think about it, not of death nor of Lena.

After running around the park being stupid, we were both pretty hungry and in need of a feed and I had some cash to pick up!

'You wanna stay over in Richmond tonight? I've got a pick up along the way.'

'Yeah, I reckon that'd be alright, long as you keep your old nana snoring to yourself.'

I went to pinch him on the arm for the smartarse comment he made, but he ran off. He made me smile, really wide. I think I was lucky that it didn't make my lips split! It had been a really, really, really, long time.

I didn't realise on that day, that Sammy would never leave my side.

CHAPTER EIGHTEEN

SAMMY BEING SAMMY

'I'll go see what I can get,' I said, waving the last ten bucks in front of Sammy's face. 'You go and...' I stopped, thinking of what order I was to give him next. 'Just stay out of trouble, beg or something, over there.' I pointed across the road to the train station exit.

'Yeah yeah A. Just chillax alright.'

I sighed, shook my head and watched Samm cross the road. I continued to watch him, not trusting that he would actually stay out of trouble. He sat on the ground right next to the exit and crossed his legs, folded his arms and looked up at me with a cheesy grin. It was only once I saw him behaving that I started to walk toward the supermarket. I was almost at the double door entrance when I turned around to see if he was still in the same spot. He never sat still. Wait where is he? I asked myself confused, looking up and down the street. Then I saw him stalking out a lady. Please don't do it, I repeated in my mind, but oh, yep, of course he did. He snatched the lady's handbag from out of her hands. If that wasn't bad enough, like a cheeky little monkey Sammy cartwheeled down the street.

'For fuck sake Samm!'

That was Sammy being Sammy. No matter how hard I tried to keep him out of trouble, it didn't work. To be fair, he only did stupid things when we were running out of money. I wanted him to trust that I would take care of it, but it was hard at times keeping us afloat. I really didn't want him to get mixed up in doing bad shit. If he got caught, they'd put him back in the system and he'd probably end up with another family that picked on him and made him feel like a petrol-sniffing loser.

You know, I don't get it, taking him from his Dad. It was after Samm's mum died of cancer. It was real quick and Samm was real young and his Dad kind of fell apart. If they had of just let him get over Samm's mum, get his shit back together, well then maybe he would have been all right. Maybe he could have taken care of Samm, but it was far too late for that now. As soon as his dad was left on his own, after they took Samm away, he killed himself. Now it was Sammy that suffered the price.

I didn't bother going into the supermarket, it was time to move on. There's not too many aboriginal boys running around Richmond, so we had to go. We had to move on so he wouldn't get caught.

True to form or habit, when I went looking for Samm, he was sitting in the park near the underpass where I had first met him.

'Samm what the fuck do you think you are doing?' I scolded him just like a mother would. I hated that about myself.

'No worries A. trust me hey. Look at all these fifties! We like rich or som'n!'

He was right, there were many fifties, but I couldn't help but feel bad for that lady. Maybe she was on her way to buy food for six kids and now they would starve without it. Or maybe she was on her way to pay her rent and now she would get kicked out and we'd see her on the streets in a week. Or maybe she was on her way to buy some bags of ice. Hmmm she didn't look like a junkie, but that's how they all started out, normal, until slowly over a short period of time they lose far too much weight, their eyes become sunken, their teeth start to rot and soon they are fucking over their best friends. Yep, we'll go with option number three. We just saved her from a life of torment that will end in her death. It always does with junkies, jail or death.

'Don't worry hey A!' Sammy said. 'I ran away.'

'Cartwheeled,' I interrupted.

'Yeah, sweet huh! Maybe I should join the circus.'

His cheeky grin was infectious, but I remained with a straight face. If he thought it was funny, then he'd do it again.

'As I cartwheeled away,' he continued, 'I snatched out the wallet, threw the bag to the side, cartwheeled again, cause you know I'm a star,' he said it as he pulled up a pretend collar, from his pretend shirt that he was not wearing. 'Then I grabbed all the cash out and dropped the wallet. No evidence.'

And with that, Sammy stood up and took a bow.

'Yeah, you're real smart,' I said sarcastically. 'So smart indeed that now we have to move areas and you gotta stay out of Richmond.'

'Small price to pay. I was bored of that place anyway.'

I rustled his head and pushed it to the side. He annoyed me, but I couldn't stay mad. He pushed my arm away and started karate chopping me. I guess the play-fighting thing, was our thing. I wanted him to learn how to defend himself without the ridged teachings of Ty. If I told him it was fight time, he'd dance around like a jerk, so it was easier to let him think it was kind of a game... fun.

Samm got us into more fights then I had ever seen in my whole time on the streets. He had the biggest mouth, cheeky too. Everyone at the start, when they first met him, wanted to smack him in the face, which was not OK with me. I had to pull the Pho card out quite a few times, which I didn't like to do. I didn't want to be associated with him. One reason because of Ty, but two, his enemies would become mine. I'll do the drops but that's it. I never dealt directly with him. I probably would have spat in his face if I saw him.

Over the next few months Samm had gotten better. He didn't get under people's skin so much. He kinda made them laugh instead. He was still stealing and that had to stop. The problem was that I hadn't had much work. M Double DM had been slow and I refused to go back to what I was doing when Ty went to prison. It wasn't just about me anymore.

BANG! Sammy got me a good one, punched me in the stomach, snapping me out of my head.

'Oh sozza A, you alright?'

Standing bent over at our favourite spot (by the tunnel where we first met), I gave him a look of 'oh please'. Fighting is more about front than power. When I go all "crazy bitch" people get scared and don't want to mess with me. It's an edge, my secret weapon. I've used it before, smashing a bottle over my head. It gave me a concussion, but those dudes never messed with me again.

'A?' Samm said, as though about to ask me a question I wouldn't like. 'Me bro's…' he was referring to other black fellas, his indigenous friends. He continued, 'over in Brunswick. Well the squat they staying at by the com center, it'll be empty.'

I dropped my guard as Sammy continued to circle me with his arms up in front of his face. 'Samm you know I don't do squats no more.'

'I know A, I know, but hear me out.' He was jumping backwards and forwards looking absolutely ridiculous. 'There's only the three of them and they're taking off out west. It's got running water, there's nothing to pay for, no one knows it, it'll be safe.'

He slapped my arm and I put my guard back up.

'The money we do make, you can save, do the caravan or som' shit. Go north like ya said.'

He had a good point. We could stash the money in a box, bury it under the squat, then head north. I hate to admit it, but it made sense.

I then made my move and kicked Sammy's leg out from underneath him and pressed him down to the ground by his chest. 'Awhhh hey!' he yelled out, more in surprise than in pain.

'We'll see,' I said.

Sammy flashed me his cheeky grin again cause he knew he had me. He knew the "we'll see," meant yes. I couldn't believe I was taking advice from this kid.

We pretty much headed straight to the squat and circled the surrounding streets.

'This is like the fourth time!' Sammy exclaimed with annoyance. 'Can we just get there already?'

'First rule Samm?'

'Know your exits,' he sulkily answered, as he kicked a stone out in front of him.

'Where are they?' I demanded more than I was asking.

'We got two to the north.' He pointed his hands out straight ahead like a flight attendant. He continued, 'two to the sides, over the fences, to the properties that open to each of the roads.' Then he moved his arms out to each side indicating the exits. 'And the back leads to the park, so it's perfecto!' He turned around and signaled behind him then chimed in a girly voice, 'your captain would like to welcome you today, please use the toilets in this bush and that bush and this bush.'

I cracked a smile but dared not show it to him. He would have gone on and on with that airline thing for hours if he thought I found it funny.

'Safe house?' I asked him.

'To the library,' he said in his most official stern voice.

'And tomorrow we'll go there and read some more,' I replied.

'No! Come on A. Can't we do something else? Like anything else. I hate reading, I can't do it.'

Same winging, different day. Ignoring him was easier than arguing with him again. He needed to get his reading up. When he turned sixteen, he could nominate who he wanted to live with and that would be me, so I was going to send him back to school. I didn't want him to end up like all the other streeties and definitely not like me.

To be honest, I had no idea why he listened to me at all. I wasn't his mother nor his sister, aunt, teacher, caseworker... I was just his friend. But for some reason, if I said we were doing something (after constant hours of whinging) he'd do it anyway. Funny hey.

The squat was no paradise, but it wasn't all that bad either. As I walked up the side path, I knew it would do for us, for now. Who knew when construction on the street was going to start, apparently it was all council land now. There was no sign of anything happening anytime soon, so I was confident we'd be gone before it began and as long as no one knew about the squat and that we were staying there, then we would be OK. No one else would come to claim it.

Sammy said his goodbye's to his bro's and went and sat in the yard, which kinda made me nervous. As much as possible we would have to stay out of view. Another rule; stay as invisible as you can. It just causes trouble otherwise.

Sammy was sitting on the back step, twirling a laminated pocket sized picture in his fingers. It was a picture of his mum. He missed her. I knew he did. Every time he had to say goodbye to someone or a place we had to move on from, he would twirl that picture as though he was saying goodbye to his mum all over again.

Samm was the funniest kid I knew, always the loudest and the wittiest. He'd outsmart every dumbarse kid on the street. I was sure there was a genius in there somewhere, itching to come out. It had been years since his mum got sick with cancer and died, but for Samm it felt like yesterday. I'm sure all the pranks and the clowning about he did, was the one thing that distracted him from his pain. I hated it when he got like this. It felt like there was nothing I could do.

'Hey Samm, you wanna get a Macca's thick shake?' I asked.

Sometimes that worked, but he barely moved and didn't say a word. I am not someone who likes to be touched and I certainly do not hug, so instead I sat next to him and put my head on his shoulder.

'We gonna be alright. You and me Samm.' I would say this to him every time. It seemed to be our routine now.

CHAPTER NINETEEN

MAKING THE DEAL

Winter friggin sucks. No electricity, no heating, barely any blankets… it just sucks! BUT we were lucky cause we were in a house. I would walk through the streets and see other streeties curled up in corners, near stations and vents, doing what they could to keep warm. No one else notices them because they are invisible, but when you yourself are one of the invisibles, then you spot each other a mile away. I wanted to tell them to come with us, that we had shelter, but I couldn't. I didn't know who they were or what they might do to us, so it remained mine and Sammy's secret.

One particularly cold night had a sharp chill in the air, so Sammy and I curled up in the front room together. It was the warmest room in the squat.

'Look at that fog hey Ange,' Sammy said, breathing out an icicle cloud.

He kept clicking the torch on and off while I thought about how far off we were from moving out of there.

'Will you turn that bloody thing off!' I snapped.

'Alright, alright, no need to get your nickers in a knot.'

Sammy turned off the torch and I rolled onto my other side.

'A?' he asked.

'Shhh,' I whispered back, hearing footsteps come from outside.

I didn't think twice. I clicked my fingers three times (our "get out" signal) and we silently jumped to our feet. I had used that emergency click only once before, so Sammy knew that it was real. We moved away from the front door and headed for our exit, the bathroom window. It was on the right side of the house and close to the fence. We had already mapped out the pathway to the road when we first moved in.

We didn't touch anything, we're not that dumb. You have to leave everything behind. I could hear the latch being tinkered with on the back door and then the pole I placed under the doorknob dropped and echoed throughout the laundry. Footsteps ran through the house as we lunged toward the window, leaving no time to check for any of the intruders outside. I pushed Samm through first and immediately followed, slamming the glass behind me and jamming the lock. We were ready and prepared for this very moment. Sammy leaped to the top of the fence and I followed swiftly, effortlessly, like a lion plunging for its prey. As my arms reached the top of the wooden boards, I fell backwards to the ground. One of the intruders had pulled me down by my leg.

'I got one of them!' he yelled out and I knew I had only seconds to get free.

I squirmed like a caterpillar trying to roll jump to its feet, but he was strong. With the palm of his hand he grabbed hold of my face, forcing it back down to the ground. I felt a sharp pain draw up through the back of my head, piercing my skull and sending warm trickles of blood down my neck. I felt dizzy and disoriented. I was not myself, the blow convincing me to give up.

Then I heard the crumble of a brick, the crack of a skull and Sammy pulled me up to my feet. I didn't glance back for we didn't have time, but I knew he had hit the intruder over the head with one of the loosened bricks. We ran through the neighbouring yard, our cleverly pre-mapped path leading us away from the scene. I had no idea who they were but they weren't there to be friends. They were there to take the house and anything else we had and then they'd leave us for dead. It happens all the time in this way of life. We were never safe, we could never just be.

We ran three suburbs over without noticing a puff. When we finally did stop and take a breath, we found ourselves in a park and I knew I had been there before. The second night I spent on the streets after Ty went to Jail, was there. The tubular structure still standing bright green, how sick of this life I was. Not enough

room for us both inside that slide, we could not hide
in there. So we climbed up and over some bushes,
curling up in the middle of the branches, waiting for
the morning to come to decide our next step. I was
absolutely sick of this life.

When the morning had come, I had not slept at all
and quietly got up to leave. Sammy was still asleep. I
walked to a phone box and dialed my contact. It was
time to setup a serious drop, make some serious cash;
make this happen. There was mention amongst Pho's
crew, of picking up a big drop cause Jimmy went to
jail last week. The idea had been playing on my mind,
as I considered if I should take it. But now, in this
new circumstance, I had to leap. You know, I once
heard a guy on this TV ad say, 'with big risk comes
big reward.' I decided this could be true for me too.
It was time for me to do this. I could make Jimmy's
drop.

Standing in the phone box, in the corner of the
park, 'yeah I can do it,' left my mouth. 'Ty won't
know. I won't tell him.' Their hesitation spelled fear
of Ty, but how could they be afraid of him? Why
would they? They worked for Pho. 'Yep, I'll do it.
OK. Bye.' Then I hung up the phone. As I turned
around, I could see Sammy walking toward me.

'Where the hell did ya go A? It's supposed to be
us! Remember!'

He was pissed off that I left him alone in the
bushes. He had bloodstains on the sleeve of his shirt

and across his shoes. The blood from the intruder I guessed.

'Listen Samm, I'm taking the big drop.'

'No A, don't do it. You'll get busted like Ty.'

'This is not the same. This is glass not guns... and it's not up for negotiation.'

I began to walk, not wanting to listen to his plea. I knew it could all turn out bad.

'But you don't have to do this,' he continued.

'Samm I want out!' I stopped and turned around.

'I want out of here, out of this. Go north where it is warm, where we can do more.'

'More what A?'

'More. I want locks on the door. I want you to go to school.'

'I don't need no school. We'll be alright.'

'I want more than this for you. I don't want to do this anymore Samm. Last night was a close call. I've had far too many of them. I've had too much of this shit.'

'Ty gets out soon A, he'll take care of us.'

'It's not his job to Samm.'

I didn't know how to explain to him how angry Ty would be when he found out that I'd been running dope for Pho. He made me promise I'd steer clear of him and I broke that promise almost straight away. Besides, I knew that I was well and truly damaged goods. Not even Ty could possibly want me.

'One last drop, just this one.' I said.

'We'll grab our cut, head up north. No one can find us there. You'll be sixteen in just over a month, you won't have to hide no more and Ty could meet us there.'

I wasn't sure if I was trying to convince Sammy or convince myself that this was a good idea. I told Samm that Ty would meet us up north for his benefit, to put his mind at rest. I didn't really believe that Ty would, especially not after this. You know I never went to visit him in jail. I only ever spoke to him on the phone. He never asked me why I didn't go. He never mentioned it at all.

'Pho's really gonna give you that much gear?'

'Well it's Jimmy's cut, Jimmy's drop, but he is in the can, so it's ours. One last run and we disappear for good. Clean deal.'

'What if they screw you over?'

'They won't. They owe Ty a favour. You think they'll screw over the girl he protected? When Ty protected Pho and his whole crew?' I hoped I was right. 'Besides, this is tactical. I'll do the drop, you collect the money, that way he knows we won't run off with either.'

'Backup?'

'We don't need it. It's one dude. I've dropped for him before. It'll be smooth, I promise.'

Sammy shot me a devilish smile and slapped me a high-five. 'Ha!' he exclaimed, convinced it would all be all right. 'We can do this A! Whoop whoop!'

I had this funny feeling in my stomach I was trying to ignore. As soon as I said, I promise, I wished I never did. It must have been the blow to my head that was making me act all weird. I started to think that maybe I had a concussion or something, so I touched the back of my head with my hand and the pain rang right through my ears. The blood felt as though it had dried up and now formed a lump.

'Let me have a look A,' Sammy said, reaching up to touch my head.

I brushed him off and moved his hand away. 'It's fine, but we do need to get cleaned up.'

There was blood on the both of us and we didn't need any more attention, not now that we were so close to getting out of all of this. There was no backing out. I had made the deal. I had to do the run.

CHAPTER TWENTY

OUT OF PRISION BUT IT'S TOO LATE

I'm not sure why they called Pho's crew's "hub" a barn, when it was clearly a warehouse. A small warehouse made of wood. When they first told me "the barn" I expected to see hay, animals too. I figured they called it a barn cause it was much smaller than your average warehouse. It kinda made me laugh cause when you say the name Pho, people shake in their boots, but his warehouse seemed more like a mini-me operation. Kind of like putting a poodle next to a German shepherd. Who the hell named Pho anyway? I mean, what kind of a name is Pho Phan Phuc? Let me tell you, it's Phucked! Sammy would have laughed at that one. I never even considered taking him to the warehouse with me. It was safer to leave him behind. I was there to organise for Sammy to collect the money in a public place, just in case something happened to me. Can you believe I was already thinking that something bad was going to happen!

Daisy's words rang through my head, 'always have a backup plan.'

Tigger rolled back the warehouse door and nodded for me to come inside. I always thought Tigger was a girly name, like he would prance across the fields. I assumed he got his name from the orange stripes dyed through his hair. He was Asian too. I think they were all Vietnamese.

Ty's half cast; half Aussie, half Viet. Maybe that's why he was taller, stronger, tougher and looked different to all of them. Like he had some tough white rough-nut man in him (not that he would know. Ty was adopted).

Tigger lead me to Johnny, who told me where I would pick up the stash. He gave me a key just like Lucy had done back in Sydney all those years ago. With that thought, my stomach dry retched inside itself. I had to push those memories down further below my tummy. There was no way I was letting those feelings out. It'll be fine I kept repeating to myself. This is your chance. This is Sammy's chance.

I put the key in my pocket and gave them a nod to close the deal and then walked toward the roller door. Tigger stopped me to whisper in my ear, 'if you screw this up we'll cut your boys neck.'

It sent a shiver through my body. I knew they would hurt Samm if anything went wrong. That's why he will pick up the money, while I do the drop.

I kept walking out of the barn, brushing Tigger off as though it was no big deal, showing no fear at all. There was no point in being afraid anyway, I knew the deal was sealed. It had to be done. There was no turning back.

As the door began rolling down behind me, I raised my eyes from off the ground, looking out toward the road. I was almost knocked over by shear shock. Ty was standing right in front of me.

'Ange?' he asked confused.

'Ty?'

I ran and threw my arms around him, melting into the safety of his familiar grip. He held me tight, caressing my head. As he pushed on the wound on the back of my skull, I let out a small yelp of pain and stepped backwards away from him.

'Ange, what's going on?' Ty said my name sternly this time. I knew that this was bad.

'I, um...' and then I realised, 'what the hell are you doing here?' I was confused!

'You haven't called in over a month. I got parole.'

'So you came here?' I said angrily, without really realising that I couldn't be his first pick because I had no address to give (not one that he could know about anyway).

'I came to pay my respects, let them know their secrets are safe and I'm here because I asked that you would be safe. I was hoping they knew where you were, but you're here. Why? What have you done A?'

'I did what I had to do.' I responded coldly, blankly. It was the truth.

'I did six years so that you wouldn't have to do this shit and now you're telling me you're dealing arms! Fuck Ange!'

'I'm not dealing fucking arms OK! I did a couple of drops. It's not a big deal.'

'You're running drugs? I told you to stay away from that shit!'

'I had to do something. You left me Ty. What the fuck was I suppose to do? Get a job? Who is going to hire me? Huh? Matted hair, stinks like shit, has nowhere to live! They seized everything that same fucking day.'

'So the job? Cassie? The place you were living at? It was all a lie?'

'What was I suppose to do? Tell you how the fuck I was making money?'

I could feel the blood boil up out of my skin. This was not how I imagined our first meeting to be. I had fantasized about it a thousand times and it always ended with us running off up north together, not shouting it out in the driveway of some mini-me barn.

'I went to jail to protect you, so Pho didn't come after you. Look at you… it's for nothing. You're going to wind up in jail or dead!'

'This is the last deal Ty. Samm and I want to head north. Start again. New lives.' You'd think I'd stop tempting fate with that line, "new life". Every time I said it, something went wrong, but it's all I wanted, to be safe, to be free of this shit. That's all any of us ever wanted. Whether you can see it or not, we want out. We do this shit to survive. I was doing this so Samm could have a better life.

'You sound like me A,' Ty said, as though he was reading my mind. 'I wanted you to be safe. Chloe died because of me.'

'Ty! This is not the same! She fell through a window.'

'Because I was fighting with my Dad. Don't you see, you want to save Sammy… you're ending up like me!'

'You're wrong Ty, I'm not going to abandon Sammy.'

And with that I think I broke his heart. I trusted him and he abandoned me. How could he possibly walk in there after six years and tell me what to do! He couldn't say ro to me. He couldn't tell me not to take the deal. It was the one deal that was going to give me the chance to have a fresh start. It was going to take us away from all of the shit. I could see it in Ty's eyes, the pain it caused him, looking at me, dirty, broken, a mess. Deep in my heart I think I always knew it was because of me that Ty went to jail. Doing that last deal to give us a new life. Staying in jail to protect me. He wasn't protecting Pho like I always thought he was. He was protecting me, so that they wouldn't hurt me. Again doing what was best for me. It wasn't his fault, he never deliberately tried to hurt me, but I was angry. I was so angry that he left me. That's why I hardly called him. That's why I never saw him in jail. I was embarrassed of what I had become, angry that he left me, angry that I had no one, angry at all the shit that I had to do to survive. I did what I had to do and now it was all too late. We couldn't go back. He saved me that day in the alley, just for me to Phuck it all up!

I knew I had to stop that shit running through my head. I had to focus on the moment I was in and in that moment I had to give to Sammy what I had promised... a better life.

Ty reached out to grab me but he stopped and looked up toward the top of the barn. I followed his gaze to a small window and there was Pho smiling smugly from up above.

'He'll never let you get out Ange. He'll snap your neck in a second without even blinking.'

'Well then come with me Ty. This was your dream to go north.'

'It's not that simple A. I have parole and next week is full of reintroduction into society shit. I have to get a job and stay steady. I need a release to change states and a parole officer to take me on. I can't just take off, not if we want to stay clean.'

'Then I can do this deal now and go. I'll get it all ready. I'll set us up. Ty you know I can't back out now. It's too late.'

Full of sorrow, Ty nodded his head. We both knew there was no turning back. It was best for me to deliver the deal then leave. Ty would be setup with accommodation anyway, a halfway house appointed by his parole officer. I couldn't stay there with him and I wouldn't leave Samm alone, so it was best that I disappeared. Then, when he was parole free or could move states, we'd be waiting. He could always get out of working with Pho until his parole was over. All he'd have to say is that he was being watched, that they wanted to catch Pho. No one wants that kind of heat, so they wouldn't use him for any more deals.

'I'll make the drop with you,' Ty insisted.

'No you won't. You can't Ty. You just got out!'

'Ange, this is not a negotiation.'

It was the same words I used with Sammy. I knew I couldn't argue.

CHAPTER TWENTY ONE

THE DEAL

I've used those words many times, 'this is not a negotiation'. Sammy knows I don't negotiate, just like I knew Ty doesn't either. What was said was going to be done, so I had to think fast. Yes I was about to deceive Ty, but it was for his own good. I couldn't have him break parole and wind up doing another six years because of me. If I got busted then I'd do two maybe three years. It was a chance I was willing to take, but I wouldn't risk Ty's freedom, he had done that for me already. Besides, once it all went down and we were on a bus heading out of Melbourne, Ty would understand... well, with a bit of time he would forgive me.

I instructed Sammy to take Ty to the money pick up point where Sammy would be given the money. I told Ty it was the drop point and that I would meet him there. I said that I would carry the backpack from point A to B on my own, no negotiations. He had to be at the parole office first to check in and there wouldn't be enough time for him to accompany me the whole way. He wasn't overly pleased but he agreed to meet at the drop point to monitor the drop and make sure I was safe. It was all a lie and completely fake. I was really making the drop on my own and Ty was going to the money pick up point. What I didn't know was that Sammy had told Ty, as they walked to the fake drop site (which was really the money pick up point), that he was not going to sit around and wait for the drop to happen, even though he knew it was the pick up point. Instead, Samm said he was going to the pick up money point, which was in actual fact the place where I was dropping the package off, which I had strictly forbidden him from doing.

So there I was walking across the Yarra River, with Flinders Street Station behind me and a backpack full of ice on my back. I was taking much deeper breaths in than usual and slowly wheezing them out, as I stared everyone down that walked past. I felt like everyone was staring straight through me and knew exactly what was in my pack. It always seems that way when you are doing something dodgy. You feel the piercing eyes penetrating your skin, when in actual fact I was just as invisible to all of those people as I was the day before. Still, I drew in another deep breath and sighed it out slowly as I continued closer toward the drop point.

Albert Park seemed as good as any other spot. There was a mini forest, full of overgrown trees. Not a bad place if you need a quick getaway. I had scoped it out the night before, making sure there were plenty of exits (and there were).

I walked straight through the center of the oval, so the contact could clearly see me (I also needed to keep a clear circle around me just in case). I could see him standing by the barrier leading into Sherwood (the mini forest I was talking about). I was OK with that, I could get out if I needed to. I knew the exits.

My heart began to race more than normal. It felt like it was squirming around inside my chest, missing a beat every couple of seconds. I thought to myself, if only you could bottle this shit, this adrenaline pumping through my veins. I could sell it for a squillion dollars. Not like I'd need the adrenaline anymore, I'd be rich, living in a mansion with a door padded thick with locks. No one would be getting in. 'Snap out of it Ange!' I yelled at myself. 'Focus!'

The drop dude was tall, built larger than me, but I wasn't afraid. I did eighty push-ups that morning, trying to keep myself fit and strong. As I reached him I called out, 'Pho,' while darting my eyes through the trees, making sure we were alone.

I threw him the backpack, which he caught with one hand. He unzipped the pack and smirked like the devil. Make the call,' I said. But he just shook his head. My stomach fell through my knees and straight into the ground. Do not show fear, anger, happiness or pain; an instruction that came quickly from inside my head. Emotions are your worst enemy. Emotions reveal your weaknesses. This was a rule when facing off with thugs. I repeated, 'make the call.'

I barely got the last word out when he had me by the hair dragging me into the forest with my legs kicking in the air. I ordered myself to gain composure and kicked my leg around underneath him. I buckled his knee and sent him down to the ground.

'Fucking bitch. Mate now!' he shouted. Then a second thug appeared. I flipped up to my feet, looking for a weapon. I knew a massive branch would do and would be easy to find. There were plenty of them, fallen, broken from one of Melbourne's winter storms. It was at that same moment I realised what Samm had done (and I was grateful for it). He came flying in with a kick, metal pole in hand, knocking the first thug back to the ground. I grabbed the backpack and told Samm to 'RUN!'

I followed him through the trees toward the back of the mini forest. The two men so close behind us, I could feel their breath on the back of my neck. We jumped up onto the fence and fell over the other side. I dropped the bag as I rolled out toward the main road. Samm was already across the street by the time I got myself back up. Noticing the bag a meter away, I leaped toward it when BAM, a bullet was fired. I sprung back in fear. I could see through the wire fence that the two thugs had a gun. I stepped toward the backpack, as Sammy yelled out, 'NO ANGE RUN!'

Without thinking clearly I did as he said. How stupid, cause now I was dead. Twenty-five grand worth of glass was in that bag and if the thug wasn't going to make the pick up cashola call, then that meant something bad had happened with the money transaction too.

Two cars pulled up, as the thugs ran away with the glass. It was Pho's men in those cars, now with guns pointed at me.

'RUN SAMM, CIRCLE!' I screamed.

Samm knew what that meant; come back to the point where we had just come from. We'd meet there. It's a tactic Ty had used to lose whoever was on his tail. No one suspects you'd go back to the same point where it all went down. But this town was small and Pho would have men everywhere. I wasn't so sure we would make it out of the block.

Meanwhile, while we were running for our lives, Ty was at the money pick up point. OUR money pick up. Tigger was there and shook his head.

'Apparently your girl has done a runner with the drugs. We'll let Pho take care of her now.'

And with that Tigger put the cash back in his jacket and Ty knew that I had been setup. Tigger had set me up. Whatever had happened, it didn't matter. Ty knew Pho would never believe me. Ty knew that Pho would kill me and he also knew that there was nothing that he could do about it.

CHAPTER TWENTY TWO

RUNNING AGAIN

As we parted ways, I heard a, 'YEHOOOO!' followed by a BANG and Laughter too! It was Sammy jumping over a fence. He loved the show of it all, thinking he could out run them, which was actually true, he could. His laughter became faint, then disappeared. I kept running, repeating in my head to circle back. Circle back Ange circle back! Lose them!

I turned left down Cecil Street. I knew exactly where I was going. I circled the park four times the night before (sometimes it pays to do your homework). Turning the corner I heard the screech before I saw the car and I hit it like a sack of potatoes, sliding across the bonnet.

As I reached the ground I sucked in some air, cringing from the pain of my knee that I grazed. I yelled at myself, 'get up! ANGE! It's not broken!' Then I pounced at the fence, climbed up to the top, rolled over the wire and jumped to the ground. My knee buckled, but I scrambled back up just as quickly as I had dropped.

Running! Always running! Someone should have tattooed it across my head. Your destiny Miss Browski is to run your whole damn life! I had come so far, I was not about to give up. I was not going to lay down and die.

I continued running down the back streets and then catapulted over a brick fence. As I neared the next corner I saw who was ahead of me and I began to back pedal like a cartoon character trying to take off, but is frozen, running in mid-air. My feet gave way underneath me and I gasped for air, trying not to make a single sound. Fucking Pho Phan Phuc! Across the road he stood as swarmy as fuck, sucking back on his cigarette. The panic set in as I struggled to breathe. I closed my eyes tight and prayed like I had never prayed before; don't see me, please don't see me, I pleaded and pleaded as I fell to the ground. I clawed at the concrete turning myself around and immediately took off back in the direction I came from. I knew there was another route, another exit strategy.

I found my way back to Albert Park, running through the long grass, back toward the mini forest. It felt as though I was running through that field all over again, the one from the very first night this whole nightmare began. When my street life began. This time no blood from my ear or welts on my body but it was just the same. Running frantically for a new life.

On that night she hated me more than ever before. She kicked me and punched me and pulled out my hair. She punched me and punched me while I sat on a chair. Swollen from the blows she dragged me to the floor, where she kicked me and kicked me, right up into my rib cage. Finally she stopped and pushed me out of the door, grabbing and ripping a chunk of my hair, forcing me to fall. I didn't stay around for more. I ran. I cried. I ran. One foot in front of the other, I kept going. I felt like I was there all over again. Fourteen years had passed since that day and I was still running.

I made it to Sherwood, the mini forest at the end of the oval and grabbed a hold of a branch, struggling to catch my breath, struggling to gain composure. No tears this time, I wouldn't waste not one, not on Pho, not on that fucking Phuc!

I noticed one of Pho's crew standing out in the distance as obvious as a red flag to a bull. Dumb fucks I thought to myself. I scurried and crawled and ducked through the branches, I knew my way out of there, but before I could get back to the wired fence, I was pulled to the ground by a hand that clasped my mouth and muffled my sound. I rolled through the shrubbery with my attacker trying to scream until I realised it was Sammy!

He didn't let go. He held my mouth tightly shut as I tried to swallow my scream. We lay there on Sherwood's floor, Sammy pressing his chest on top of mine, trying to control my erratic breathing. We could both see one of Pho's crew standing just a few feet away. I could see terror in Sammy's eyes.

There was a second crew member out in the distance, who whistled to the guy closest to us and nodded him in a different direction, but we didn't move. We lay still, staring at each other.

'Pho's gonna kill us!' Sammy squeaked out as silently as he could.

THIS IS FUCKED flashed before my eyes, in big ginormous red letters. I didn't know why I was so surprised, as it always turned out this way.

'Fuck him Samm!' I blurted out.

'We gotta meet Ty, he'd know by now. We gotta get ou'da here!'

'We need that money!' I barked back.

'Ya got the pack?'

I looked at Sammy with anger and pure frustration that said, you know I don't have the pack! He was pissing me off!

'We gotta go A,' Sammy said, as he cautiously moved away, staying low while inching forward.

How did it all get so fucked up? I questioned myself, as I lay there on that forest floor. What went wrong? There was something missing, but who...

'ANGE NOW!' Sammy roared, snapping me out of my head, as he pulled me up onto my feet.

'Why weren't you with Ty?' I yelled at Sammy as we ran down Spencer Street.

'Really? Now? Let's just get to Ry's!' he hollered back at me.

This was our contingency. If everything got messed up, just get to Ry's, a cafe dive not far from Spencer Street. If all went well and the deal went through, then that's where we would say our goodbyes.

As we drew near, I could see Ty in the distance nervously smoking a cigarette while pacing up and down the footpath. I had been hoping this was going to be a happy good-bye, that we would say to each other, 'great work! I'll see you soon.' It was suppose to be a moment with Ty. My moment with Ty.

Sammy and Ty were supposed to be together, waiting for me with the money. I was supposed to walk up to them smiling. Ty a little annoyed that I lied, but happy that it all went down OK. Then Sammy and I would board the bus and wave to him from the back window. There would be no tears, mostly because I don't cry, but also because he would join us soon and we would all be together; a new life for all of us. Why couldn't it just happen like that?

I sprinted the last stretch of road, barely able to breathe. As I reached him, Ty flicked his cigarette away. I stopped and bent down, struggling to catch my breath.

'This is fucked up!' Ty said.

'I got setup!'

'Fuck Ange!'

'Fuck Pho!' I screamed. None of this was helping.

'You gotta go and you gotta go now. I can't protect you A.' Ty shook his head in disbelief. 'You sent me to the wrong spot. I could have stopped all of this.'

I wanted to scream it out of my eyeballs, I fucked up again! WHY! WHY! WHY!

Ty handed me two tickets and said, 'these will get you to Sydney. Be careful there.'

But all that went through my head was, Sydney! Fucking Sydney! You know how much I hate that place. He handed me a piece of paper with his mobile number on it and said, 'I'll come to you.' Then he hugged me like it was our final goodbye, like he knew something that I did not. He held my face into his neck and I held onto that moment in my head, as though I was taking a snapshot picture. I opened my eyes and the moment seemed to last forever. We stood there staring at each other. It was as though I had never imagined it happening but had been waiting for it all of my life. It is the only true moment of feeling I have ever had. The only spark through the darkness I have ever felt.

'Ahh shit!' came out of Sammy's mouth, breaking the moment as Tigger and Johnny stood across the busy road staring right at us.

There was no time left for thoughts of Ty, we had to take advantage of the cars passing by. Tig and Johnny were blocked by traffic, so Sammy grabbed my arm and started running. We ran up past Ry's and through the back alley. With just a few minutes to reach the bus, we jumped over bins standing in our way, but my knee buckled and I headed toward the ground, Sammy catching me as I fell.

'I'm fine. Come on!' I said, as I shook him off.

My knee was throbbing but we had only a minute or two to get to the bus before it left. We pushed through the crowds and headed straight toward stand C, as the double doors on the bus began to close. Sammy stopped them by jamming his arm through the middle. It was a God moment. If I believed in him, I would have said thank you.

We showed our tickets and headed down toward the back of the bus. Sammy spotted Tig outside the window and immediately pulled me down to the floor. My heart was racing from a mix of fear, anticipation and sadness. I couldn't breathe in case Tig saw us.

We held our breath on the floor of the bus for what seemed like forever, not relaxing until we rolled out of the station. We carefully moved up onto our seats, making sure we had not been seen. I was so scared of what they would do to us if they caught us, but I also felt sick to my core with the thought of returning to Sydney... and worse, I didn't believe I would see Ty again.

So we sat in silence staring at each other until we hit the highway, until we knew we were truly free. It was only then Sammy sang out in true Sammy style, 'piece of cake!'

CHAPTER TWENTY THREE

ARRIVAL

It was all too familiar, coming into Central Station early that morning. I felt a chill as I remembered thirteen-year old me. I reminded myself that I had to keep every single memory buried if I was to survive that town.

We had barely any money, a few coins between us. It was enough for a couple of bus rides. I hated that situation. I'd been in it way too many times before with no money, no place to go and on the run. I wondered what normal twenty-six year olds were doing? Not this shit that's for sure. I hated it. I hated me. I hated…

'Yo A, snap oud of it,' Sammy said, snapping his fingers in front of my face.

'Just thinking… what next,' I replied.

'Well I'm hungry, so how about Macca's?' Sammy chimed, clicking his fingers maraca style while doing an excited little dance. He really wasn't worried at all.

I looked up and down at the both of us. Me with dirt stained on my hands, under my nails and all over my top. Sammy wasn't too bad, but we both needed to get cleaned up before we did anything else. Plus there were cops all around Central Station. They were making me nervous.

'We need to get cleaned up, find somewhere to stay, get something to eat. I know a place.'

'What no Macca's then?' Sammy sulked.

I said nothing, no response. I just pulled on his T-shirt toward the local buses. I was taking us to Bondi Beach. I knew it well. I used to shower in the public block at the Pavilion. I hoped it was still there. It was the one place that was free and safe. I could wash my clothes and myself all at the same time.

We got off the bus on Campbell Parade and walked down toward the beach. Waves were smashing against the shore, pushed there by the windy air. All the beautiful people ran past, trying not to look at us.

We approached the Pavilion from the back. The hill was covered by grass spreading all the way down to the cream building. Samm spotted a cardboard box, setup as a shield from the wind. Behind it a homeless man trying to keep warm while he took a nap. I don't know if it was because no one else noticed us, that all us homeless did notice each other. Sometimes I felt like we attracted one another like some kind of secret pull, something that tied us together. I called us the invisibles because let's be honest, we felt invisible,

people treated us like we were invisible and sometimes, I felt like being invisible and disappearing altogether. As I continued walking down toward the toilet
block, I noticed I was walking by myself. See! I was
even invisible sometimes to Sammy too! He went to
bum some cigarettes from the man behind the box.

The shower block was pretty much how I remembered it, deep troughs, good for stomping on clothes.
I could wash them old-fashioned style. Us streeties
didn't have the luxury of washing machines. Now
that would be a treat! Ty and I had a washing machine
back in Melbourne and I would wash my clothes every single day even though they didn't need it. They
smelt like flowers and sunshine whenever I lifted the
lid. I really loved that.

The tiles in the block were grimier and dirtier
than I remembered but hey, wasn't my whole life like
that. I took off all my clothes except my undies and
let them drop to the bottom of the shower. I quickly
picked up my jeans cause they would never dry on me
(it was way too cold for that). I covered the drain with
my T-shirt, creating a small bath. I found a piece of
soap lying on the floor. It looked like it was years old,
but with a few twist and turns the suds ran off and it
was like new again. I began to lather my clothes.

It was times like these I missed my home with
Ty. What we had wasn't anything special, but it was
home. Our home. I had my own bottle of liquid soap,

delicious coconut, almost as though you could eat it (which I don't recommend). I tried tasting it once and it certainly did not taste like it smelt (and no I didn't do it because I was hungry, we had food back then :-).

I loved how it smelt on my skin. I'd sniff my arm and hands randomly throughout the day. It was a happy time. I was able to pretend that nothing existed before my home with Ty. I was pretty good at doing that.

I heard the giggles before I saw the girls. Four of them about fifteen or so years old, walked into the shower block. They laughed and pointed at me like I was nothing but one big joke.

I felt like screaming at them, YOU THINK I LOVE WASHING MY CLOTHES IN THIS PISS ARSE DIRTY TROUGH YOU SPOILED BITCHES, but I didn't. They don't care. It would be a waste of my time. Instead I wrung out my clothes and put the wet pieces back on, the whole time staring them down. They were scared of me and I had nothing to lose. If they decided to touch me or try and hurt me, I was already building up inside of me for the psycho bitch to come out for her show. Just by having the will to do something bad is enough to scare people away. Truth be known, I was more afraid about what everyone else was going to do to me then what I was capable of doing to them.

As I left the bathroom I hissed at them and just like that, they retracted into the wall, avoiding my stare, feeling afraid. They let me go. I walked straight out of there.

Outside Sammy was waiting for me.

'I'm starving!' he said, while staring at my wet T-shirt.

'We gotta find a squat Samm.'

I pulled the coins from out of my pocket and jingled them in the palm of my hand, counting how much we had. There was enough money for two bus tickets up to the Cross. I hated Kings Cross. We used to call it KX back in the Lucy days. KX was our best chance of finding a squat and I was hoping that the bakery I used to know was still there and still gave food away at the end of the day. It couldn't have changed that much, could it?

I grabbed Sammy's hand and we walked back up to the main road.

I knew Bondi fairly well, but my memory was a little jaded. I was doing my best to remember the things that would be useful to us, but at the same time I was trying to block out all the bad shit that went down there.

'I think there is a fruit shop around that corner,' I pointed out to Samm. 'We'll run round, grab what's out the front, circle back through the next street and come out over there, straight to the bus stop, OK?' It was a brilliant plan.

'Ha ha yeah A!' Samm said with delight, rubbing his hands together like a kid who was just about to buy some lollies on his way home from school, after finding a buck in the gutter.

'Alright, let's do it. Go!' I ordered.

And with that we ran across the road dodging through the traffic, a car or two beeping at us. We rounded the corner and could clearly see the display full of fruit outside on the footpath. Jesus! Watermelon! I thought to myself. As if that wasn't the hardest thing to eat.

Samm and I looked at each other, nodded and then the final kick of adrenalin shot in, plunging us forward like bullets flying out of a gun. I had no idea what Samm had picked up and it really didn't matter, anything was good! Me, I grabbed a quart of watermelon and kept on going through to the next street, sprinting without looking back. I legged it across Campbell Parade, between two trucks and caught sight of the Kings Cross bus pulling up to the curb. Samm was head to head with me and we waved at the bus to wait. We boarded, paid our fare and the bus was off. No questions asked. No one followed us. No one probably even saw us. We high-fived each other (how could you not!). That was a supremo effort!

Sitting down the back of the bus Samm threw an apricot at me and I threw the watermelon back at him, swapping what we had. YUM, I really liked those apricots. Sweet and delicious like a tangy pear but with firmer skin. I scoffed it down real fast while Samm bit into the watermelon, spilling juice everywhere. Still he smiled. It was a win for us. Ha ha! Take that hunger! Another point to us! The scoreboard wasn't in our favour but today we weren't going to be beaten.

As we sat on the bus eating our score, I thought about how I was going to explain KX to Samm? I'm not, I decided. I was going to take the silent clause, like the Fifth Amendment (I wasn't even sure what that was but neither did Samm... so I win!).

CHAPTER TWENTY FOUR

KX

We got off the bus near Kings Cross Station. It was like a cold shiver not only went up my spine but also struck the center of my brain, as though it was searching for memories, the ones I had buried so far away. I once read this thing about a hippo something... campus maybe? Hippocampus? Anyway, it's basically where you store your memories and you can improve the function of it. I remember when I was reading about the hippo I stopped. Why would they teach me that! No way I wanted my memories back, so I threw the book in the bin (library bin. It wasn't mine). Anyway, there I was doing my best to bury the memories. I didn't want to bring them all back. No thanks!

KX was heaving, as it always was. Not much had changed from what I could see. Same coke sign, same junkie asking for money, strip clubs, same, same, same.

'So how we gonna find a squat in this?' Samm asked me.

'I know where we can ask,' I said, cause sadly I did know. I knew these people, well not these exact people, but I knew where other streeties would hang. I used to sell drugs there.

Under the overpass was where the invisibles met, hung out, slept, dealt drugs. We kinda weren't all that invisible down there. We'd call it the bridge. It was sort of a hot spot for police to come hassle ya. But you know, safety in numbers and all that.

We walked down Brougham Lane and it reminded me of the meerkat. Swallow it Ange, I told myself, swallow it now. I gulped and we continued down that long stretch of road, toward the base of the road bridge.

I caught a glimpse of myself in the reflection of a house window. How different I was to the girl that had arrived there thirteen years ago. Taller, stronger, fully dreaded hair. I kind of looked scary, unapproachable. That little girl in the reflection was scrawny, pale, matted hair, lost, afraid.

'So whad ya reckon?' Sammy asked.

I had no idea what he had said.

'You're on my bad side, remember deaf ear,' I said it as I tapped my left ear.

It was true I did have a deaf ear. Never regained sound in my right ear. However Samm was standing on my left.

'Is that so?' And with that he came up to my left ear and shouted, 'shame I know it's ya right ear!'

I pulled away cupping the side of my head.

'OK, OK, you got me!'

'Ya didn' hear a word I said.'

'Sure I did.'

'Well then, what I say?'

'Ah here we are!' I grinned, knowing that I just got out of whatever it was that he was saying. I hit him on the chest (which was actually more of a pat) and motioned him toward the underpass. He grunted like I had annoyed him. I did annoy him. I think we regularly pissed each other off. What else did we have to do? Gotta lift the boredom somehow. Sure beats drinking or taking drugs, although it was getting harder to keep Samm away from booze. The more he hung out with other fellas, the more they pushed booze in his face. It wasn't just them, most kids on the streets were drinking... it's hard dealing with all of this crap. Sometimes you've just got to roll with whoevers around otherwise you end up alone.

It was just as I had remembered it, under the overpass. A concrete jungle with old mattresses, rubbish, a few bums sitting against the massive pillar. A hideous roar came out of one of them, as he missed his mouth trying to swig liquid from a bottle. The perfect candidate to ask an important question like, where's a squat? He'd be loose enough to spill the beans and then he'd forget he even told us. That way he couldn't tell anyone else that he had sent us there. No one would follow us.

'Hey you!' I called out.

'Mesh?' he said, wiping the rum or whisky, or whatever that brown stuff was from off his chin.

'Where's a squat round here?'

'Squahsh? You want to play squash?'

'Squat. Shelter?' I pronounced slow and rounded.

'He too pissed Angie, ask someone else.'

Samm was right, he was hammered, way past the loose lips stage and well on into the drool phase. Something told me he didn't move from that spot often and probably didn't remember anyone ever talking about a squat. I think it was his feet wrapped in newspaper that made me think that. Not good for walking, but perfect for keeping warm. I kinda felt sorry for him. It gets real cold out and he didn't even have any shoes. At least we had shoes.

Then with a hideous roar he continued, 'ha ha ha hash…' coughing his guts up, 'haveshnt plashed squatsh in yearsh.' Then a screeching hiccup popped out of his mouth. 'Excusesh me!' he exclaimed, then took another swig from his bottle, this time gulping it down.

'Samm, pull out the ciggies,' I instructed.

'I've got like three!'

'Pull em out Samm.'

I knew this was the only way to attract other streeties. Rare to have money and everyone was looking to bum. If they could get a free ciggie they would. If we could attract one, then perhaps we could get an answer to a squat, although I didn't like the idea of anyone knowing where we were gonna stay.

As Sammy pulled out a cigarette and lit it up, I thought about our plan. I knew that once we had found somewhere safe to sleep we would have to get out of Sydney as quickly as possible and to do that meant money. We had to have money. I had to come up with a way to make money.

I turned around and noticed the old drunk guy passed out and his bottle of booze slightly falling over. He probably spent his last dollars on it, his only comfort in this shit life. I bent down and moved his bottle upright so that no liquid would spill.

'Hey mate, you got a spare ciggie?' I turned around and sure enough a streetie about the same age as Sammy was approaching us. Very reluctantly Sammy answered, 'yeah' and handed the kid a cigarette. The kid lit the cigarette and then breathed it out through his nostrils like a dragon. My eyebrow raised slightly but I lowered it just as quickly as it popped up. I had to act cool. No extra attention needed and I didn't want him to remember me for any reason. Better that way. If he came across anyone... if he mentioned us or something to the wrong people, they'd know that we were there and maybe where we were staying (that's if he told us a place), it's just best not to be remembered. Not me anyway.

'Do you know a squat round here?' I asked.

'You guys new in town?'

I didn't really respond, just sort of gave him the chin, like it could have been a mistake that I moved it or I was giving him the nod that he was right. It was a tool I used to avoid answering questions.

He continued, 'there is one on Church Street. Up round the corner. Mainly used for sniffing but the cops cleared it out last week. Pink building. Number two.' He then nodded toward Sammy, 'you got another?'

I gave Sammy the eye, you know the eyes that say, 'I'll kill you if you don't do it,' but your eyes don't move at all. It's like tellapathy or telly something, pethy, pathy? I don't know what it's called but its like two minds connect and Sammy knew not to say no. We had to give that kid another cigarette. We had to keep him on the happy side, as he knew where we were gonna stay.

Sulkily Sammy handed him his last ciggie and the kid walked away.

'See, I told ya I'd find us something,' I said, proud and happy with myself. A wins a win right? Probably the only praise I ever got was from me. It had to come from me otherwise I'd get no praise at all.

'Why'd we have to give him the last ciggie?' Samm complained, but he already knew the answer. It was his way of telling me he hated what had just happened, but of course I already knew that.

'He knows where we're staying.' I went to ruffle Sammy's head but he ducked out of the way. It was then I noticed a drug deal going down across the road.

It was after all my turf, my old turf where I also used to sell drugs. There was nothing out of the ordinary, nothing at all unti_... my heart stopped! The cold in my face, my neck, my arms, it froze me, as all of my blood drained from my body and forced itself into my toes. I'm surprised I didn't vomit in that very moment, instead the word 'FUCK!' Projectiled out of my mouth.

'Who's that?' Samm asked.

The guy, thin, same rough wild hair, who almost saw me! Was distracted by his junkie. I instructed Sammy to 'RUN!'

How could this be? How could this happen? The very first day I see him! My insides wanted to turn themselves inside out and leap far away and out of my skin. We ran up through the back streets of KX, I turned like a million times, praying to the Godless being somewhere in the sky that Jase didn't just see me. My heart was bashing its way to the outside of my chest, contained only by a slither of skin. It was beating in my chest so hard, fighting to lock everything from the past in. There was an internal fight between the importance of locking that shit away and the necessity to pump blood through my body. How could I explain this to Sammy? I was never going to talk of my past. He could never know. I was not going to tell him. I was not going to tell anyone!

We reached the top of KX and I bent down behind the corner of a brick fence. I peered in the direction from where we came. No Jase. He had not seen us. He had not followed us. Thank you! Thank you to a Godless sky, to a God that did not exist.

We kept walking, trying to catch our breath. I knew where Church Street was, but all I could think about was how shit just got complicated. I knew I couldn't show how sick I felt or show any of my fear to Sammy. I had to be strong. I am strong.

'Who we running from A? What ya look so worried for? I'll kick his arse!' And with that Sammy started his, "Eye of the Tiger" routine, humming and punching the air. He pounced backwards and forwards, jabbing in the air to the beat of, 'duh... duh-duh-duh, duh-duh-duh... duh-duh-duhhhhhh.' I wondered if he had even seen Rocky the movie?

As we came to the corner of Church Street, I looked up and sure enough a faint spray painted number 2 was on the opposite building across the road. The entrance was shut and bolted, but I already knew that wasn't the entrance. Had to be the tree that reached the second floor window. That meant we had to wait till dark to climb inside.

So that was the squat done. Tick. Next we needed to find some clothes to sleep with, food, money and above all, stay out of sight from Jase. Just another day in the life of Angela Browski! I knew I needed a new plan, a better plan, but really I had no idea what to do. I wanted to ask Ty, what do I do? I wasn't sure why I thought of him, I mean I lived without him for years...

but I didn't want to go back to doing the things that I had to do when he went inside. No not again.

Sammy was still pretending to be Rocky, throwing a couple of short kicks, high kicks and some rather questionable punches. We should have been sparring again. Helps pass the time. He did almost make me laugh as he hummed "Eye of the Tiger", but I knew better than to laugh cause he'd be doing it all day and all night if I did! And although Eye of the Tiger, is a "classic" song -a hundred times later it's bloody annoying!

'We'll have to wait till it's dark.' I paused, not sure of the next instruction to give. Jase hadn't seen Sammy, Jase didn't know Sammy, so he was safe around KX. As long as he kept his mouth shut, then he would be all right. 'Don't talk to anyone, but see what you can drum up for food. Stay low. When you get back, we'll wait it out over there.' I pointed across the road, the perfect spot to sit and take watch. Three exits in case I saw Jase and comfy enough to sit. We'd see him before he'd see us.

Sammy nodded and headed off in search of food. It was my turn to find stuff to sleep with. I knew a spot I could head to (if it was still there that is). I knew I had to stay out of sight, but I also couldn't sit still. More importantly, I had to find a way to score some dollars. Our timeline got shorter as soon as I saw Jase. What are the friggin chances he was still there! Still alive too! I felt like it was as rare as finding five hundred bucks in a bin. Maybe I should have rummaged through a few different bins, although the luck seemed to work in reverse. Me the bad luck, everyone else soaks up my opposite, good luck.

It felt risky walking the streets again, but I couldn't just sit there and think about all of things Jase would do to me... had done to me. It's weird, I hadn't even thought of Pho with all of the Sydney crap coming back up. With all of this shit inside me and going on all around me, I wondered if death would be better than living like this? When I left Sydney all those years ago I was dead and then I was renewed. The renewed me wasn't whole. I never completely bounced back. Then Ty went to jail and I was on my own... and now? I'm just here, neither dead nor alive. I think it was Sammy I lived for.

CHAPTER TWENTY FIVE

WHAT CAN I DO?

First stop for me was clothes, blankets whatever I could find. Charity clothes bins were perfect for that kind of thing. The more you get, the more comfy the floor would be. What? You didn't think we had beds now did you? If you're staying in a squat for a while, then you might locate a mattress from somewhere (street throw outs and stuff like that). Nobody spends money on a mattress when you gotta eat (or have a drug problem... no judgment here).

So I was doing my thing, flung over the side of a Vinnie's clothes bin. It's real hard you know, having the circulation in your arm cut off because you're buried so deep inside the big tin thing, trying to grab a hold of something, anything, while the lid presses into your arm. It's kinda like a lucky dip, who knows what you'll pull out! You'd always hope you scored something cool like some trainers or a big woolly blanket and at the same time, hoping no one chucked any sharps or broken shit in there. People do dumb shit when they're bored and don't give a shit about us streeties putting our arms inside, getting all cut up and shit. Sometimes that happens.

So basically while you've got one arm in the bin, the other arm is holding the round lid thing open as wide as possible so you can reach in. Talk about make it hard for ya! Don't they know we need this stuff? Anyway it's like being a bloody acrobat at times. It's easier with a stick and someone else to hold you up.

So, I was up on the side of this bin, stomach muscles tensed so tight they were popping out me belly, but keeping me in place as my feet locked onto the side of the bin. Bloody tough work! I flipped my fingers around in circles hoping to lock onto a bag and BINGO! I got one. I scraped my arm along the edge of the lid as I pulled it out, simultaneously I jumped off the side of the wall, almost losing my arm as the lid came clashing down! As I hit the ground and turned around, there was some stupid arse white boy staring at me in his clean jeans and collared top. Definitely a rich kid.

'What cha lookin at!' I spat at him.

'Ahh, um, ah nothing,' he stuttered out in response.

I dropped my shoulder and rammed right past him. Gotta show him who's boss. The dumbarse just kept staring at me (he was asking for trouble). Lucky I'm not a psycho like some of the others (well not as much of a psycho). It did piss me off, him staring at me. I wanted to scream at him, what? You think I like doing this? It's so I have something to sleep on rich boy! My blood was boiling and I didn't know why... this kind of thing happened all the time. My rage just got worse when I walked across the road and found Sammy chatting away to some aboriginal guys. He would always call them his "bro's".

I threw the plastic bag full of clothes at Sammy. He caught it and shook his bro's hands, then fist bumped them and nodded (a sign to say, later bro's).

'Samm!' I said, dragging him by the arm away from the street. 'They aren't your bro's!'

'Jesus A, why ya got ya knickers in a knot? They are me bro's, relax A.'

Telling me to relax was like waving a red flag to a bull, not that I'd ever seen that, just read about it in a book. I was finding it hard to control the panic that was welling up inside of me. I was so friggin scared that someone would know Jase or even Pho. I had to keep us safe long enough to get some money together. I was about to lose my shit.

'We gotta lay low for a couple of days. So don't talk to anyone alright?'

'OK, OK.' Samm threw his hands up in defeat.

We walked silently back to the squat where I stashed the plastic bag by a tree and sat waiting for darkness.

I couldn't sit still any longer. Ants in me pants syndrome. Plus the more I sat with nothing to do, the more time my brain had to remember the things that I didn't want to remember. I had to move.

'I've got an idea,' I said to Samm. 'Wait here OK? If you get a chance when no ones around, climb up.'

'Yeh,' Sammy said lighting up a cigarette, which he must have got from one of his bro's.

'Where you going?' he asked.

'Money!' I raised my eyebrows up and down at him, giving him a smile that said, I have a plan!

I headed back down toward the main street. I knew it was dangerous to walk around with Jase floating about, but I decided that he hadn't seen me and he didn't know I was there, so really I had the advantage. I had the upper hand. If I was careful and stayed out of sight, I could look out for him, run before he had a chance to see me. Samm and I could be out of Sydney real quick, without him ever knowing we had been there at all. If my plan worked and we got a good score, we could be on a bus that very day.

Embedded in the buildings, I retracted into invisibility and walked along a side street to the bottom of the hill, where I knew there was a clear escape to the wharf. It's the perfect place to throw wallets overboard. I didn't rob people often, but I knew where and how to do it if I was desperate.

The pharmacy was the perfect spot. People always had money going in there. They would go to the bank and then the pharmacy before doing their giant food shop. Sometimes you could get a wallet with three hundred bucks! That's two tickets to Brisbane.

People get distracted in pharmacies. They're waiting for a prescription, so they put their wallet in the shopping basket that's flung over their arm or the basket is sitting cn their hip. Either way they aren't paying attention to the basket and what's in it. Even the ones who cru se the aisles without a basket, end up putting their wallets down on the bench at the register because their hands are so full of the crap they are buying. Now you've gotta snatch the wallet real quick and you gotta run real fast and empty the wallet as you escape, then throw the evidence away. You shove the money down your pants and hide until the coast is clear. Most of the time people just want their wallets back, but sometimes you get a guy who wants to be a hero and won't let you go.

So I walked into the pharmacy and had a look at the tampons. No one bothers you at the tampon aisle. No one even asks if you need any help. It's like a secret code between females; I'll be quick, but no eye contact, not necessary for us to acknowledge that I have my period. And the guys? Well, they are scared and embarrassed. It's written all over their faces; is she on her period? Will she go mental at me? What if she asks me about the absorption rate, oh I'll go red. Best to just leave her alone and not to ask. She knows what she is doing.

It's the perfect scope out cover! And the longer you linger, the less likely they are to come over, cause then they'll have to offer advice and no one wants that.

Now I'm not proud of the next moment, but it was necessary for my survival (Samm's life also depended on me getting us money to get out of there). A pregnant lady who was almost about to pop had her hands full and a basket too. She dropped it all on the countertop and some fell on the floor. She then placed her wallet next to the register, an edge really close to the door. As she turned her back and picked up what she had dropped, her arm knocked over some jellybeans. Hmmmm jellybeans, rumbled through my mind and my belly. I really loved those jellybeans. My favorites were... SNAP OUT OF IT ANGE! I screamed at myself and refocused my eyes on her wallet. I ran past the counter, snatched the wallet and escaped out the door.

I ran as fast as I could, not looking back, then I opened her wallet... Damn it! There was no cash inside. I threw the wallet away, just meters from the store.

I could hear a boy yelling out in the distance from behind me, so I legged it even faster down toward the wharf. As I reached the bottom of the hill and approached the waters edge, I leaped like superman across the wooden stairs, crashing behind one of the blocks and landing at somebody's feet. As I looked up to see who was at the other end of the feet, I noticed it was that same stupid arse face staring at me again!

The same one from when I jumped off that Vinnie's clothes bin.

'Really!' I rubbed my head into my hands. 'Look dude I didn't do nothing!' I could see the recognition coming over his face. He looked over his shoulder and then back at me, as I lay there down at his feet.

'What did you do?' he asked me.

What a stupid question I thought to myself. Clearly it was something dodgy, but like I was going to tell him that. I mean DAH!

'Nothing man,' I pleaded.

I thought I was pretty convincing until I noticed a chocolate bar or two that I had also ganked at the pharmacy, had spilt out of my pocket.

'Come on man, I didn't do nothing. That guy is gonna hurt me. You have to help me.'

'Talk to me and I won't tell them you're here.'

'Them? Wait what?'

I started to get up but immediately dropped back down cause there really was two of them. Shit! I had nowhere to go.

The dude, whose feet I was lying at, turned to the two guys and was about to yell out to them when I hit him in the foot stopping him.

'Alright man. OK!'

I agreed.

CHAPTER TWENTY SIX

THE OFFER

We sat down at a café near the wharf. The two guys were long gone (I made sure of that first). I had no idea what this guy wanted to talk to me about, but I figured if I had the opportunity, I'd grab his wallet and run. After the last Fail (yes with a capital F), I had to try something else... and this guy? Well, he had a gullible face.

'So what ya want?' I finally asked him.

'You were pulling bags out of that charity container and...'

'So!' I snapped back at him, letting him know that his stupid comment pissed me off. I mean, what was he going to ask me next? Do I love it? Yeah it's awesome (not!).

Distracted by the waitress, he turned to her and asked for a flat white. A flat white! Pompous prick. You mean a coffee with milk. Probably cost him five bucks too. I could feed me and Sammy on five bucks. Two-minute noodles if you can heat the water up or a can of soup. Five bucks worth of chips, two pies, or a loaf of bread and jam. Yet this tosser orders a flat white!

'Would you like something?' he asked me.

'I don't need your charity,' I said as the waitress continued to stare at me. 'What you looking at?' I snapped at her. Why do people always have to stare? Is it OK to stare at someone in a suit? Or someone really fat? What about a little kid? Or any other customer? NO. So don't stare at me! The douchebag (I decided to call him douchebag cause he had really pissed me off) handed the menu back to the waitress and she scurried off from whence she came. Whence! What a stupid word. I learnt it in one of the Shakespeare books Ty borrowed from the library. I mean are you kidding me Ty! Why give me a stupid book like that! When the bloody hell would I ever use that kind of language? Oh right, yeah, now... I just used it. Maybe I'm the douchebag!

'I'm putting an article together and I thought...'

'You thought what?' Douchebag.

'Maybe you could tell me about the streets? Why you were running from those two guys?'

He said it so nothingly, like he was sitting drinking tea, asking me to pass him the Sunday paper.

'You're fucking kidding me!' I exclaimed.

As I stood up to leave he added, 'I'll pay you. One hundred dollars.'

'I don't think so.' left my mouth, but Sammy and I needed that hundred bucks.

'Tell you what, you think about it,' he said as he began to write his address on a piece of paper. 'It's just a few questions. Come by tomorrow and we can talk.'

As the waitress placed his flat white (coffee with milk) on the table, I grabbed the piece of paper and ran. I ran because I wasn't sure. I mean, there was no way I would trust the guy or tell him anything about my life. Why would I? So that other people could laugh at me and tell me how bad I've been? No way! But I grabbed the address anyway. A hundred bucks wouldn't get us to Brisbane, not by bus nor by train, but it made me think, if he was willing to throw a hundred bucks my way, how much money did he have?

My brain went into overdrive, like there was a little mouse inside my head, turning a mini wheel of ideas with it's tiny little feet. This could be our ticket out. I could steal some of his stuff. It was pretty obvious that the sandy haired guy, with really blue eyes and dimples in the side of his cheeks, had plenty more money where he came from. Someone once told me, you can tell a lot about someone by their shoes and it was true. That drunk guy under the overpass had his feet wrapped in newspaper, I wore runners (hey I was always running, made sense) and the douchebag wore black polished leather shoes, laces that looked like silk. His shoes alone would probably pay for two tickets up north. He could afford to lose a pair of shoes, right?

By the time I got back to the squat it was getting dark and Sammy was already inside. I climbed up the tree as fast as I could and jumped inside the window.

'Hey nice one!' I called out to Samm, who had arranged newspaper and clothes on the floor, ready for us to sleep on. We'd be staying warm that night.

I threw Samm one of the chocolate bars I stole..

'Nice one you!' he said and began chopping on the bar.

Chocolate was Sammy's most favorite thing. OK well chocolate and Macca's. Sammy wore the same T-shirt everyday with LOVES CHOCOLATE printed across the front. Pretty funny cause he did! It was the one thing he always stole, the one thing he was always being chased down the street for, the one thing he would die for! He needed to learn to sneakily grab a bar or two instead of the whole shelf!

I threw him a second bar to soften the blow, as I wasn't too sure how he would react to the douchebag thing. Actually I lie. I knew exactly how he would react. He would hate the idea.

'Samm,' I said quietly, endearingly, finding the right words to convince him to follow my plan.

I think he knew something was about to come out of my mouth that he wouldn't like because he made a very long drawn out, 'hmmmmm' noise, while still chopping on what was left of his chocolate bar.

'I've got a plan,' I said as I moved myself to the floor and began my pushup routine. I had to stay strong. I really should have been sparring with Samm. It was always the first thing Ty would do with me when he got home from one of his trips. He said I had to be able to defend myself and get myself out of whatever situation I was in. He was right. I've used his tactics hundreds of times, saving my arse and Sammy's more times than I can count.

'I met this guy, well not really, that didn't come out right.'

Talking made push-ups so much harder, that's why I always did them with Samm around. Fighting and running came hand in hand. I had to be able to do both and win. If there was ever a time I needed to do both, it was in KX on the run from Pho. I needed to keep fit. I needed to keep me on my toes.

'His gonna pay me to answer some questions for some thing.'

'Sounds stupid to me.'

'Hundred bucks!' I squeezed out, as I continued with my push-ups.

'Sounds too good to be true.'

'Nah, I think he's one of those do-gooder types. I figure...' I started to strain trying to push myself back up.

'If he's stupid enough to ask me to his house, then I'm smart enough to steal all his shit. We need cash. We gotta move, we've got a few days max.'

'What's the hurry?'

I stopped to get my breath back.

'Trouble found us Samm. That drug dealer… and Pho… it's not safe for us here.'

'How'd ya know him?' he asked me.

That dreaded question. I didn't allow myself anytime to think. There was no way I was delving into that image, that memory, not for anyone. 'It doesn't matter,' I responded. 'We just gotta stay real low and head north… that means mula.' I gave him the dollar sign, rubbing my fingers together. If there was one thing that spoke Sammy's language, it was mula.

'So ya really gonna help this fella out?'

'No! I'm stealing his shit and getting us outta here.'

I got up and headed over to Sammy and started making makeshift pillows, scrunching up some newspaper and rolling it inside a jumper.

'Trust no one, stick together. Screw them before they screw us!' That was our motto and I wanted to make it clear that it was just Samm and I. This guy meant shit to me. It was a meal ticket. Samm then gave me a whopping high-five! That was our agreement handshake. No shaking, just slapping.

I settled myself onto the newspaper and tried to roll into comfort, which wasn't working at all. It was like lying on a plank of wood that had been wrapped in concrete and paper machaed without drying properly, leaving it wet and smelly. I think it was the walls. Mould probably. Still, I had smelt a lot worse so I didn't complain.

'OK roll it,' I told Sammy.

'Really we have to do this every time,' he whined, followed by a massive sigh and then continued with, 'water tap outside at end of the block. Nearest toilet at the station or next to the tap at night,' he gave me a cheeky wink. 'Found metal bar in corner of room,' he pointed to the far side of the room. That was a check for a weapon (just in case). He then added, 'the window is the only exit cause that door is bolted shut.'

Hmmm, I hated that there was only one exit.

'And Samm, if shit goes down, our backup spot is Brougham Lane, that first street we came up.'

God knows we needed a backup. Scratch that... I knew we needed a backup. I was listening to Daisy's lesson; always have a backup plan.

CHAPTER TWENTY SEVEN

HOPE

I woke up earlier than Samm. There was nothing unusual about that, but I couldn't shake the sick feeling that was welling up inside my stomach. It was the sick feeling combined with noisy garbage men outside that woke me up. It was still dark, so it must have been in the fives. It's the life really. I was used to it. It didn't mean that it didn't suck. If you had shelter that was safe, you could stick around and sleep-in, but in most cases we were up in the fives. Wake-up early and move on before you got caught or found, then go snooze in the park later when there were lots of people around. It was probably different for older guys, but as a girl or a young boy, you gotta stick to the numbers and hide during the night and stick to public places during the day (the safe spots to sleep).

I got up and pumped all of my sick energy into more push-ups. I felt like I was becoming a machine. A push-up crafted robot. I missed sparring with Ty. It had been such a long time since we were together, a lifetime ago really. That sick feeling, that weird uneasy energy I was feeling, was all because I was back in Sydney. It was bringing up a bunch of stuff I didn't like.

In Melbourne, Ty always made sure I was fit and able to look after myself. I stopped training so hard after he went inside. The more I pushed myself, the hungrier I got and that's not good for anyone, not when you've got no money for food.

'Ange, why don't cha' give it a break,' Samm said, rolling over rubbing his eyes.

I jumped to my feet.

'Come on, we gotta go, before it gets any lighter,'

Good ol' crusty'o Sammo! He's everybody's best friend, but not in the morning!

We left everything in the squat as it was. One, because we were going back there later that night and I couldn't be bothered resetting all the newspaper and clothes as our bed. Two, if anything got stolen, we didn't care, the clothes came out of the bin. And three, I took note of exactly where everything was and then placed the metal bar across the windowsill. If anything moved we'd know someone had been there and that it wasn't safe for us to stay. It could be anyone, sniffers or cops, even Jase... just not safe.

We walked to Bondi Junction, where there was a massive shopping centre. It took about thirty minutes and Samm complained the whole way. We were hungry. I'm really snappy too when I haven't eaten.

The large supermarkets are bright, glary and not easy to steal from, especially in the morning when they are empty and all the staff are out stacking shelves. The smaller fruit and veg shops aren't so bad. Sammy hated it, the green stuff, but this particular little grocery store we went to, was located in the bottom of a car park and had croissants, cheesy scrolls and even Cheese & Crackers in tiny packages. All yum! I managed to get them all under my jacket and walked straight out the entrance instead of the exit, where no one was looking or waiting to check your bags. It really was a piece of cake. Delicious too!

So breakfast was done tick. We called that lunch as well cause I knew we wouldn't eat again until I got the hundred bucks off the douchebag. Then we headed to the library cause I needed to use the toilet and find the douchebags address on one of their computers. I told Sammy we'd relax in the chill out corner (every library has one), flick through some mags and stay out of the weather. I told him it was going to rain that day. I had no idea if it was or wasn't going to rain, I just wanted a safe place where I knew Jase wouldn't see us. As if he'd ever go to a library.

Keeping busy was sometimes one of the hardest things. I couldn't force Sammy to read and I'm not sure why I did read when Ty brought home all those books. I guess I believed back then that perhaps I could make a better future for myself. I didn't believe that now. I knew I was doomed, but why should

Sammy have to suffer with me? I could get him to a safer place, away from all the trouble. We just had to disappear and never come back. I was hopeful wasn't I?

'I don't know how long this will take today, so remember the bakery I pointed out? The one with left over bread and stuff? Lots of streeties go, so get in early,' I told Samm, making sure he knew the drill before I left him.

'How ya know all this?' Sammy asked me once again.

I really had not told Sammy anything from my past. We didn't know all that much about each other from before that day when we first met. I mean, I knew about his mum and his dad, but really that's it. I didn't know what school he went to or if he had any friends. Sammy being Sammy, I am sure he had loads of friends. The class clown, definitely not the teachers pet.

'Let's just hope they still do and not too many people know about it.' I ignored his question and he didn't pursue it either. Unspoken code I guess. If you don't get an answer (especially the second time round), don't ask again. Only us streeties know that.

The douchebag's house was old brick, nothing modern about it and really close to its neighbours. It was a city house. His place wasn't too far from the squat and I figured it would take about ten minutes to walk back later. I was feeling apprehensive about going inside the place. I don't know why. I mean, I knew I was strong and I had a knife in my pocket (don't ask... I've got to carry one) and I scoped the place out for what felt like hours. No one coming and no one going. No cars, no people. I considered for a split second that perhaps I should have let Samm come with me, but then a flash of him pissing on a couch came across my mind. It was years ago when we first met and we were staying in a hostel. The guy behind the desk called him stupid, so he acted like a monkey, scratching his armpits and pissed on the couch. I knew it was better that I did this type of thing on my own. It'll be fine, I convinced myself.

'Hi. Come in,' he said.

He held the screen door open and smiled at me flashing white, like he'd been brushing his teeth with bright light toothpaste for hours. So clean they were. I couldn't help but brush my tongue over my teeth. They were furry and gross. I hadn't brushed them since we fled Melbourne.

I poked my head inside the door to ensure it was safe. I decided it looked OK and took a step inside, keeping one hand in my pocket, holding onto the knife. I didn't trust him no matter how much he smiled, but a hundred bucks is a hundred bucks and as long as it didn't become a "clothes off" party, I was going to stay.

'I wasn't sure you were coming,' he said, motioning me to follow him through to the kitchen.

I guess it was getting pretty late in the day. Still I had to check the dimwit out, make sure I was safe to go inside. I also had to find his place without having my own computer or a phone. I also had to find and use a toilet, steal some food cause we were starving, make sure Sammy was safe and that we were off the streets so neither Jase nor Pho could kill us... but hey, I guess it was late in the day.

As we walked through the hall, passing by the front room and into the kitchen, I couldn't really tell if there was much I could take, not unless I stole the TV which was way too hard. The place looked like it was 1970's I think. I remember our kitchen in Melbourne (the place Ty got for us), it had a kitchen just like the one I found myself standing in. Ty called it 70's retro. Whatever that meant.

I sat at the kitchen table and next to a laptop. I was sure I could sell that! I wondered how much a laptop would go for? Would a pawnshop take it? They had really hardened up. You need ID to sell them stuff and they actually check it. We'd have to find a dodgy one, which I was pretty sure we could in KX, otherwise another streetie would have to sell it. Only problem with that, they always take half.

'Would you like a coffee?' he asked.

'Don't drink it,' I said. Can't say I'd ever had it before. Smelt like shit, well not shit exactly, that actually smells pretty bad. It smelt more like something went mouldy then you heated it up, left it in a cup for a week, heated it up again and stuck it in my face. Just like my mother's breath. She'd scream in my face with her coffee breath.

'So what ya want to ask me?'

'I thought I could ask you some questions about your background?'

'For what?' I asked, not liking where the questions were headed. All that shit about my past was tucked deep down into a little vault, stuck to the wall of the cave, in the empty space inside my chest.

'An article I'm writing on surviving the streets.'

'Why? No one gives a shit.'

'HELLO?' A voice called out from the other room.

Who the hell is that? Rushed through my mind in a panic. I always worry when two people I don't know are in a house with me alone. Before I could say anything, the douchebag ran out of the room.

OK! Don't panic I told myself, focus on what you can take... what can I take? I looked around the room and fixed my eyes on the back door (an exit). I could get out quick when I needed to, so I searched the room for anything I could sell, but the cupboards were basically empty and the draws were too. The whole kitchen was basically empty! The China was too hard to take and the appliances didn't even look like they would work. Then BINGO! A bowl on the countertop with loose change and a gold ring, score!

I put it all into my pocket. I considered not taking the laptop, but I was pretty sure I'd get more for it than the hundred bucks the guy was offering me. So yep, I decided to take it! I grabbed the laptop headed straight for the back door, but DAMN IT! It was locked! I turned so quickly the other way that I tripped over my own feet and went flying, hitting the floor. Like true legendary style, I saved the laptop, but let out a scream in the process. It all happened so fast, I had to think quick. I was running on the spot. It looked like some kind of stupid dance, as I panicked about getting out of there.

I put the laptop down and decided to head out the front door in a rage, that way no one would stop me cause they would be scared I was going to snap. Remember, psycho bitch worked every time!

I walked into the front room, in my fake built up panicked rage. A tall blonde headed pompous dude was standing right in the way of the door, with the douchebag standing next to him. It can go bad real quick when you're locked in without a clear exit. I told myself, 'think Ange, think!'

'What ya looking at?' I spat at the tall dude.

Not waiting for a response, I dropped my shoulder and bulldozed past him and out the front door. No one followed me.

I ran all the way back to the squat and was actually damning myself the whole way. We needed that hundred bucks. If I had the laptop, then fine, no worries, but I was coming back empty handed, except with a little bit of change.

When I got to the front of the squat I stopped and counted the coins I stole. There was enough for two McHappy meals! That would make Sammy happy. Like I said, chocolate and Macca's... he'd die for it! And with that thought I did a little dance inside my head without actually moving my body at all. At least I had one piece of good news.

When the coast was clear, I climbed up the tree and jumped through the window with ease. Sammy was sitting against the wall, bending a photograph between his fingers, suggesting something was wrong. I knew it was the picture of his mother as soon as I saw the brownish tinged backing.

'We scored today!' I said excitedly, hoping it would get his mind off whatever he was worrying about. I pulled the gold ring out of my pocket and continued, 'I don't know how much we'll get... Samm, what's up?' I asked, as I sat down next to him.

'Been stuck in here while the cops out da front.'

'Did you get any food from the bakery?'

'Nuh. I'm bloody starving! Where's the cash?'

'Some arse rocked up. Had to bail.'

'I didn't know if you were OK A. You were gone for ages.'

'I look after me-self. You know that.' I gave Sammy the gold ring, thinking that should cheer him up and then continued with, 'we have enough coins for Macca's!'

Sure enough a smile came sweeping across Sammy's face.

'Ya shoulda opened with Macca's!' he cheekily cheered at me.

We both jumped up with our tummies rumbling and acted all stupid with excitement. As we turned around to head toward the window, it was like my worst nightmare twisted itself into a fist and punched me in the throat. I gulped for air, flying backwards without actually moving at all. I seemed to do that internal dance a lot.

'Well, well, well, look who's in town!' Jase chimed, smiling smugly. 'What ya doing here Angie? Where's Ty? What, no Tyrone to protect his little Angela?'

This is why I hated having only one exit. A locked door behind me and an open window behind Jase... getting through him was the challenge. I repeated to myself, two against one Ange, it's two against one.

'She don't need Ty to protect her,' Sammy said, advancing toward Jase.

'Ya reckon ya gonna protect her, Abo boy?'

It all happened so quickly, like if I weren't living every single second in a fearful slow motion, I wouldn't even remember it.

Sammy took a step forward but Jase knocked him down to the ground just as quick.

'Awhhh, need Mummy to hold your hand?' Jase said in a whiny voice. He then spat on Sammy and looked at me, 'you have a score to settle.'

He grabbed my arms tight and rough.

Flashbacks of memories poured out of me like a pulsating light. I screamed, forcing the beams out of my body and through my mouth. I kneed him so hard I felt his balls suck right back up into his pelvic bone. I could see Ty's face and with one swooping move (Ty's move), I kicked his legs out and pinned him down to the ground.

'That's right arsehole. Ty taught me to fight!'

I spat on him while he lay on the floor, wondering where his manhood had gone. He was going to need a map to find that shit again.

'Let's go Ange!' Sammy exclaimed, grabbing me by my arm and pulling me out the window.

We ran down Church Street and up through Williams; street after street until we were deep in the dark city. I couldn't help but feel that this was now really really bad. Jase would be after us. Not just me, but us! That meant Sammy too. He knew we were in Sydney; he knew I was in Sydney. It would take just one phone call to find out why. That angry fuck face would stop at nothing to hurt me.

I didn't know what to do. The only thing we could do in that moment was find somewhere safe to sleep for the night.

As we came up Kent Street, I remembered a park by the old church. It would be quiet and dark. I didn't realise until I got there, that it wasn't a church no more. They'd turned it into an apartment block. I wasn't sure if that meant the park was now unsafe but we had nowhere else to go.

We curled up against the steel picket fence, in behind the garden bed. It was out of the wind and I hoped it wouldn't get much colder. In the distance, away from us, there was a man sleeping on a bench chair. He was our only threat until three drunk guys falling over themselves (being total dicks), decided it would be fun to taunt the sleeping homeless man and kicked him in the head.

Sammy then asked me, 'who was that guy Ange? How does he know you?'

'Shhh!' I belted out in an almost silent hurried rush. But it was too late, they spotted us and once again, 'RUN!' came flying out of my mouth.

I was sick of running and I was literally running out of options fast. Behind the Quay was the only other place I could think of for us to go. Something well lit and bright, more populated than the park this time.

In the middle of the Quay (Circular Quay), the Harbour Bridge sat to the left and the Opera House to the right. We headed to the row of shops where four dumpsters sat by another donation charity bin. Samm went to open the lid, wanting to jump in amongst the clothes but I sternly said, 'no Samm! Kids die in there.' And with that, thoughts of Lena flooded into my head. I wanted to weep. I felt so weak inside, so exhausted, so ruined from all of the gathering information that had been buried deep into my hard drive, a secret location with no password attached. It seemed like the hackers got in, Jase got in and it was twisting me apart.

'Here,' I called out while moving one of the dumpsters away from the wall.

Sammy squeezed in behind it. I pulled some larger garbage bags out that were filled with rotten food and seeping slimy liquid stuff. I piled them up so no one would see us sleeping. It stunk which was good... it meant no one would come near that spot.

As we sat behind the garbage wall, I asked myself, would it ever end? The constant running, the struggle for survival? What hope did we have? I wanted to give up.

CHAPTER TWENTY EIGHT

I HAD TO ASK

But I didn't give up. What was wrong with me! Why did I have to keep going? Finding solution after solution that never actually worked. Today's solution found me standing across the road from DB's house. You know the douchebag? It happened while I was walking and thinking. Walking to a safer spot, thinking about how this all got so messed up. We escaped Jase the night before, but for how long? Jase had been alone, but I had to ask myself, what about next time? What if he had a whole crew? I had to do what I had to do. I had to ask DB for that money. It may not get us to Brissy, but it could buy us a bed in the meantime.

As DB opened the front door, I could see in his face that he didn't expect me to show up on his doorstep.

'Hi, what are you...'

I cut him off, 'do you still need those answers?'

'I do,' he said.

He held the door open for me and I remember thinking that he was a gentleman for doing so.

I'm so weird sometimes. I guess I thought that way from watching old movies.

I walked into the front room and he offered for me to sit on the couch, so I did. It smelt like old people. Do you know that smell? It's really hard to describe, like everything you own is a hundred years old and no amount of washing will get it out. I guess I couldn't really talk, I'm sure I stunk... I did sleep with garbage the night before. DB's face got all scrunched up as I walked past him. I guess he thought I stunk too. I felt my cheeks go red. That had never happened to me before... going red.

'I didn't expect to see you again,' he said.

'Can you pay me first?' It was more of a statement than a question. I needed that cash. We weren't going to sleep on the streets that night.

He handed me a hundred bucks and I noticed there were more fifties in his wallet. I needed an opportunity to take it and leave. It looked like it was enough to get us out of Sydney.

'What ya wanna know?' I asked.

'What's your name?' he asked me back.

'Lisa.'

'Do you have a last name?'

'Pennyworth.' It just came out. Old habits I guess. The floodgates had been opened, so the old fake me came pouring out. The dumbarse then asked me the most stupid question.

'Why are you homeless?'

BOOYEAH, give this guy a gold medal! Journalist of the year cause he asked the most stupid double-barreled question EVER. Turn that shot gun around dude and blow your face off please.

'Cause it's awesome. Best way to live,' I responded sarcastically.

'Where do you sleep?'

'Anywhere I want.'

Could you imagine actually telling this guy where I slept last night? Yes the reason why I stunk of mushed up rotten apples crossed with mouldy cheese and the stench of off bacon, is because I slept with a wall of garbage around me so no one found me and attacked me.

'What about food?'

'Take what we can.'

'So you steal?'

Genius! I thought to myself. Amazing investigative question number two! I had already given him a gold medal, so I guess it was time to give him a Mars Bar instead!

'What ya reckon?'

He persisted with another stupid question, 'what about getting a job?'

And we have a trifecta! I felt like saying, yes it's as simple as getting a job because soooo many people would hire me with no ID, no bank account, no home, no change of clothes, oh wait and no experience except for pharmaceuticals. Maybe I could sell Panadol!

I was about to give him a serve of good ol' Ange's rage of stupidity, when the phone rang in the other room.

'Sorry, won't be a sec,' he said, as he set off toward the kitchen.

I took that golden opportunity and cleared out his wallet, leaving his house just as quickly as I had arrived. I almost felt guilty putting the fifties in my pocket. He had been so trusting, so inviting, yet he got so under my skin, like a creepy crawly that just didn't belong there. Irritating me. Itching me. Making me want to scream. Nah this was good, I told myself. This would get Samm and I on a bus to Brisbane and I'd never see him again!

And with that I smiled.

CHAPTER TWENTY NINE

LIZZY

'Three hundred bucks Sammstar! Two tickets to Brisvegas!'

I put my hand out to the right and he slapped it, we reversed it, we even bumped fists, then we laughed at each other. It felt like a glorious day walking up Brougham Lane, toward the train station. As we neared the end toward the light of the coke sign, that's where I saw her crying.

As if reading the future Samm said, 'leave it Ange, we're oud'da here.'

As those words left his mouth, he knew as much as I knew that I couldn't just leave it. I turned around and walked over to the girl crying by the lane.

'You alright?' I asked her.

She was hysterical and didn't move. I checked her arms and sure enough track marks. Junkie. I almost got up to walk away, but because she was so young I didn't think is was her doing. I had seen it many times before, heard the stories, almost fell prey to it myself. Remember the meerkat? In the box of mouldy sandwiches and that squared carpet? Ewwhl, the thought gave me shivers and a mini bomb exploded in my tummy, making me want to vomit. No I couldn't leave that girl alone.

Between sobs, she managed to say, 'he said he was going to help me, but now he says I owe him money. I have to work it off or he'll kill me.'

And this is how it worked in the Cross. Young blood. Get them in, trick them, pretend you care. Tell them the drugs are for their own good, give them a shot before they realise it's even in and wham, addiction, paying off debts, being a prostitute for them. It happens all the time, girls as young as twelve. Made me sick. I was not going to let it happen to this girl. I couldn't walk away.

'Fucking pimps. How much do you owe?' I asked.

'Two hundred. He said he would look after me.'

Of course he did that fucking prick, that's what they say, they manipulate you and turn you into a whore. Scum of the earth... and no one cared that this happened. Well I do!

'Ange!' Sammy pleaded with me.

I wasn't listening to Sammy. I was going to help her.

'You ran from home?' I asked.

She nodded back at me.

Fresh meat I thought. They always get them.

'What's your name?'

'Lizzy.'

'Come with me Lizzy. I need you to show me where he is.'

I pulled her up by the arm.

'Samm, help me pick her up.'

He did. Reluctantly.

Samm hated that we were about to lose our money because he knew what I was going to do. Pay off her debt with that scumbag pimp and put her on a train home. That's if she had a home and if they were missing her. She should have a chance to go back to them, if she wants to. That was never an option for me. I never wanted to go back there, I couldn't, but I didn't want this life of mine for her either. She should have more than that.

It all went down pretty quickly. Lizzy showed me where the Pimp was; a slimeball looking man, with hair covered in olive oil. Meerkat number two. He was a pig. He bumped the figure up to two hundred and fifty, as 'interest,' he said.

I knew I was saying goodbye to our first real chance of getting out of Sydney and getting off the streets for a night. I also knew I was risking my safety, which who really cared about that? A whole bunch of shit had already been done to me and still I wasn't dead. But Samm, I was risking his safety and for that I felt bad. I tried to remind myself that he was tougher than I gave him credit for. But after this stunt, I knew I was starting to wear thin on his nerves. I hope he knew we had to do it, that I'd find another way for us.

We stood on the platform at the station and watched the train roll away. Warning bells were ringing from the moving train, the stationmaster was on the PA system requesting all people to stand clear of the platform.. and us? We were standing there motionless, watching our last fifty bucks disappear, along with Lizzy, on her way back home. Sammy didn't say a word. Instead he kicked an empty can at the train as the carriages passed us by, letting his anger ride away.

CHAPTER THIRTY

IS PRISON SO BAD

So there I was, back where Lisa Pennyworth began. It was dark and as we stood across the road from the youth shelter on Crown Street, the one I ran from all those years ago, I wondered if the same people still ran the joint. There was no way they would remember me. It was so long ago.

'We don't need to stay here.' Sammy said, as we crossed the road.

I ignored his plead.

'Why ya have to give her our last fifty bucks? She wouldn't have helped us! Why help a skank…'

'Samm! I was taken.'

I stopped right in my tracks. I had never told anyone that. Neither had I snapped so viscously like that at Sammy before. I never had a reason to. We never spoke of our past and I guess I was only just realising how sensitive mine was to me. I escaped that day with the meerkat, but only just. I didn't want Lizzy to face a fate that I could have helped her escape from.

We remained in silence as we walked to the door.

And Sure enough as we reached the front door, there was a sign posted, 'full for the night,' but I wasn't going to sleep next to a garbage bin again and we weren't going to sleep in a park. What had happened with Lizzy was a total surprise and kind of knocked me off my feet. I knew Sammy was just as surprised cause I always put him first, but something about being back in Sydney changed me. I needed a little more time and staying at that shelter would buy us just that. It would buy us safety for one night. I felt like I had been saying that to myself since I was twelve. A twelve-year-old should not have to find a place to sleep each night. I should have been in school, playing with my friends, playing tiggy or some shit.

I shook my head and told myself to shut up! Thoughts like that were stupid. Fourteen years of stupid.

I banged on the door of the shelter, alerting a security guard who came over and opened the door. We walked inside and waited like he instructed. In all the years gone by, not much had changed in that place. I didn't remember much, but what I did remember was the lino leading to the office window. It was the same muddy brown that was definitely not the original colour. The big glass wall still stood strong. It must have been doubled layered or something, I mean for sure someone must have tried to kick it in. The office was behind it and to the left the common area that contained a couple of plastic chairs and a bookcase. I wondered why the chairs were plastic when they had a heavy bookcase made of wood? I mean, people go crazy, it's the nature of drugs, booze, no home, being internally pissed off at the world and everyone in it. So plastic chairs I got, throw them and they don't hurt so much, but that bookcase? That could go through a window or somebody's head.

A weedy man wearing a moustache appeared from behind the glass wall and said, 'all the rooms are full. You can register in the morning however there is a waiting list. Some people don't show up, you could get lucky, but tomorrow I'm afraid.'

I felt like asking him, afraid of what dude? We are the ones who'll be sleeping on the streets. We should be the ones who are afraid, not you! I wanted to grab his stupid little mustache and rip it off in one fell swoop. It looked like it had been stuck on with glue.

'It's just for tonight,' I pleaded with him, simply because I had no other choice.

'I'm sorry,' he repeated.

You will be! Ran through my mind, then I quickly buried that thought. I needed no more trouble.

'Come on Ange, he don't care. Let's go.'

Moustache man blinked his eyes down ever so slightly. I knew Sammy's words affected him, so I looked around for ideas.

'What about those dudes?' I asked while pointing at two guys curled up on the common room floor. I felt like saying to him, yeah that's right! I saw them!

'Exceptions to the rule… just like you I guess.'

And with that we won! He let us stay.

He proceeded to go through the rules; out when he leaves early morning, no staying a second longer. Keep it quiet, go to sleep, stay on your side of the room and tomorrow put yourself down on the list.

We took our places on the floor away from the other two guys, then the moustache man left the room. He disappeared behind the safety of his double-glassed wall. I wondered if it was bullet proof? But really there'd be no need, it's not like many people had guns, not homeless ones anyway. We couldn't afford it.

Samm and I kept to ourselves, leant up against the wall, but I swear it's as if trouble sticks to me like flies stick to shit. One of the kids on the other side of the room started to call out to me.

'Hey, don't I know you? Hey you! I'm talking to you.'

I closed my eyes and turned away from him, hoping he would get the message. Firstly, I didn't want any trouble to start and then get kicked back out onto the street. And secondly, I didn't recognize him, so either he got it wrong or he was friends with Jase. Either way it spelled trouble and we didn't need it.

'Check out this chick,' he said to his mate, forcing his attention our way. 'She thinks she's too good for us.'

'Let it alone will ya,' Samm called out.

Then the rumble began.

'I'm not talking to you abo,' the boy said, jumping to his feet.

And like true Samm style, it went backwards; well he went backwards, not Sammy but the other dude. Sam pushed him pretty hard directly onto his mate.

'Come on then!' Samm yelled out.

'SAMM!' I tried to grab him before the kid's punch knocked him over but I was too late. The kid then advanced toward me, pulling the bookcase over. See! Told you that bookcase was a dangerous piece! He frothed at the mouth and reminded me of my mother, that evil bitch. I hadn't thought about her in years. But with that thought I went crazy. Remember the psycho bitch trick? Well, I repeated in my mind over and over, 'bring her out, you gotta bring her out and scare those guys away.' I kicked and I punched and the security guards had to come and break it up, to which I yelled out to Sammy, to 'RUN!' He wasn't sixteen yet, so they could take him away. It was better to let me take the fall. Samm did as I said and disappeared out the front door. The security guards held me and the other guy down, waiting for the police to arrive.

My cell was small, the seat even smaller, made from a hard thick plastic. It wasn't a bench and it certainly wasn't a bed, so the only way you could sleep was sitting up. There was blood smeared on the wall, probably from a drunk who got into a fight. Fluorescent lights glared really bright while rude cops wouldn't shut up about what they thought of me. I could hear them talking in the distance. I wanted to scream out, 'a record doesn't tell you shit about who I am!' But what would be the point? They don't know me, they don't care about me, I was a homeless girl that dragged them out of the office and made them do more paperwork. In their eyes I broke the law, the why's don't even matter.

They kept me in longer than they needed to, to teach me a lesson. Once the lesson was taught (or so they assumed), there wasn't much else they could do; we were two youths fighting it out. It didn't stop them from taking my picture and finger printing me too. I never carried ID with me, but it was pretty hard to hide from a fingerprint when it was attached to the end of your hand. Remember the night Ty got arrested? I was in custody for days while they confirmed who I was. So now they have my name and fingerprints on file, along with a record of my affiliation to Ty (and Pho for that matter). Once they decided I wasn't doing anything else wrong, they warned me about spending time with convicted crooks and then they let me go. The youth shelter banned us both, which I didn't give a fuck about, we weren't going back to it anyway (but nice to know you have no options huh!). No charges were filed so that was a plus. I got some grueling questions about being in Sydney and my affiliation to Ty, but really there was nothing else they could do. Besides what had just happened in the shelter, I hadn't done anything wrong (not that my record showed anyway). They had to let me go.

One thing I did realise that night in jail (when they were emptying my pockets), I hadn't called Ty. The scrunched up piece of paper that was shoved into my pocket, I hadn't opened once. That had to be the first thing I did. He must have been so worried about us.

CHAPTER THIRTY ONE

REALLY?
THAT'S YOUR PLAN

The next day they released me before the punk-arse that started the fight. I never did find out if he actually knew me (I doubt it). When I walked out the double doors of the police station and onto the streets of KX, I saw good ol' Sammo sitting across the road on the curb, waiting for me.

'Hey Samm!' I called out and ran over and sat down next to him.

'Ya right?' he asked.

I just nodded. I was glad I was released, happy to see Samm, but pissed at how things went down. I was relieved things weren't any worse, but still it sucked.

'They charge ya?'

'Nah,' I responded.

'What now?' he asked.

I took a deep breath in and looked up at the sky as though searching for answers somewhere in the clouds.

'Pawn that ring?' was the only thing I could think of.

'Need ID. I can ask one of those bro's? Maybe they can hook me up?'

'Fuck,' I kind of whispered as I cupped my eyes like a child who believed if they can't see you then no one else could see them too, like when you're playing peekaboo.

'Forget going North A, what's the big deal?'

'Next time Jase will have his crew.' That son of a bitch was never going to rest until he had me, especially since I downed his arse. Man that felt good!

'What's the deal with that fella?'

No way I was ready to answer that question. The memories from the past were whirling around in my head, driving me crazy. I felt like I was going to fall over or be sick everywhere all of the time. My heart raced, I couldn't sleep, but I had to internalize it all. For one, if I lost my shit we were never going to get out of there and two, what would happen to Sammy if he saw that I was truly scared? He'd make a stupid decision that would get us both killed or him in juvie. I just couldn't let it go down that way.

Now I'm not saying that I am a smart girl, but if there was one thing Daisy taught me, it's just to do it better than anyone else. Now the douchebag (I was starting to wonder what his real name was), the one who let me into his house twice, had three hundred bucks in his wallet, a laptop and from what I could see two other bedrooms full of stuff. It was clear to me that he was a rich boy and had plenty of money. If he were missing a few items it would be no big deal. He could buy it again anyway.

I figured that he already gave me like two chances so maybe I could con my way in for a third time. You know what they say, third times a charm. I just had to be clever about it, pull on the heartstrings. I was running out of options and to be honest, it was probably our best (if not our only) option. If we used this guy, I knew we were fairly safe. I mean, if I turned up on his doorstep, what would be the worst he would do? Tell me to get stuffed? I'd still be on the streets, which was exactly where I was standing anyway. He could call the cops, but he's just not that type of person to hold you down waiting for them to arrive (I can read people like that). Plus three hundred bucks is a sniff in the wind for him, so I could go back.

It may have been the stupidest plan I had ever come up with, but I had to get us a safe place to stay no matter what. Yep, I decided it could work. I didn't have to lie completely just bend the truth a little. Like I took that money for Lizzy, that there was nothing else I could do, that he helped me save her, which was kinda true. Everyone loves a good sob story. I would tell him that I felt real bad for running out and not telling him, and that I wanted to make it up to him by answering all of the questions he had for his article thing and that I would give him back his money the next day. By the time tomorrow came, I would have already taken his stuff to offload and we'd be well on our way out of Sydney. Man if it could work!

It may seem bad what I was doing, but to me the elaborate lie (act, play, whatever you want to call it), meant food. It equaled food, shelter and money, which all equated to safety. We'd be well and truly hidden at his place and in a day or two we'd be on our way to Brisbane. Yep, I knew it was the right thing for us to do and I knew he had a mobile phone cause I saw him use it, so I could call Ty. It was the perfect plan for us. Yep! That was my plan. We were doing it.

'Samm, I've got a plan.'

CHAPTER THIRTY TWO

YEP
HE BOUGHT IT

We were standing at the back laneway entrance to the douchebag's house. I really had to learn his name in case I actually called him douchebag to his face, which he really was a douchebag if he was to let me stay at his place.

'OK, so the plan is?' I asked Sammy, making sure he had listened to me.

'You go in, spin ya rah rah rah, I wait here or not too far away. When it's dark I'll jump the fence and you'll meet me at a window out the back or...' Samm jumped up to peep over the fence. 'My mistake, I squat down by those bins in the corner till ya get me.' He smiled, then tapped his feet and took a bow.

Like always, I did not smile back as to not encourage him, otherwise he'd rock up on the back doorstep tap dancing us into trouble. I wonder if he thought I was a sourpuss old bitch? Never laughing at him. Maybe I was.

I stood on the steps out front of DB's (douchebags) house. I took a deep breath in and knocked on the door, questioning if this plan would actually work? Would he really be so trusting? Is he that dumb? It kinda made me feel bad. I guess I felt a bit sorry for him, but I had to push that out of my mind. There was a job to be done and that was to keep Samm and I safe. That's it. Nothing else.

The door swung open and behind it stood DB wearing a T-shirt that was kind of a shirt. I don't know what you call it but it's something in-between. I imagined he always looked so effortlessly manicured with his messy but neat hair, casual but dressy jeans. It's like he always looked perfect. The privileges of money I guess.

'Ah, thanks Tom. I'll review it and get back to you.' DB said into his phone and then he hung up.

'What are you doing here?' he directed at me, floored by my appearance on his doorstep.

'I was in the neighbourhood and thought I'd stop by?' I said it as kind of a joke.

He was looking out beyond me, as though making sure no one was behind me and that no one could see me at his front door. Typical. Keeping up appearances for the neighbours. Can't let them see you have a homeless girl at your door.

'Returning three hundred dollars?' he sternly said.

He looked real pissed. I wasn't sure that kind, inviting smile from yesterday would let me in the door.

'I can explain,' I pleaded.

He looked over my shoulder again and reluctantly held the door open for me to come inside as he said, 'well explain.'

I stepped inside into the hallway and he shut the screen door behind me. I took a deep breath in and let the sob story out.

'I'm really sorry. It wasn't for me. It was for my friend Lizzy. She was in trouble. I had nowhere else to go and I didn't know what to do. This guy, a pimp, he drugged her and was going to force her to have sex with all these guys to pay him back the money. It's a scam that happens to newbies on the streets.'

DB sat back on the arm of the sofa, shocked, processing my words. 'Are you serious?' he asked, genuinely surprised and concerned.

Yep. He bought it!

'I wasn't going to rip you off,' I continued (which was a lie), 'I swear' (another lie). 'I didn't know what else to do.' I guess that sentence was semi true cause I had no idea what else to do.

'Why didn't you go to the police? Put this guy behind bars?'

'You don't get it. He's in with the cops, there's this whole underworld thing going on and if I didn't get that money to her, he would have killed her or hurt her for sure.'

'How could this happen? Is she OK?'

'Thanks to you. You saved her.'

'Where is she?' he asked.

'She got real scared. Told me she was going back home.'

'I never thought that sort of thing happened here.' As he said it, I really believed he didn't have a clue about this sort of thing. Do people really not know this happens?

'Look man, I'll pay your money back, answer the rest of your questions. I can get it back to you tomorrow. God's honest truth.' People love that word. Like if I say God, then it's real. People are suckers. God doesn't exist.

'Thanks I guess,' DB said with confusion of why he was grateful.

I continued, 'I just got one problem, I kinda ticked off the wrong people and I got to lay real low until I can pick up your money tomorrow. I need ah... I need a place to stay.'

'Here?' A look of surprise and you're totally mad, swept across his face.

'Just for tonight. It's all cause I helped Lizzy.'

'Um I, I don't...'

Another deep internal breath and I told myself to lay it on thick. Heartstrings Ange, remember heartstrings.

'Don't worry about it. I'll sleep in the park.'

'It's just, well, it's not exactly my house.'

He said it with guilt, like he was unsure to say yes, but he also knew he should say no.

'It's cool, I'll see you tomorrow with your money... you've already saved one life.' I turned away from him and said drearily, 'you don't have to save mine too.'

'One night?' he asked as a statement, that it was to be only one night.

'One night.' I responded. Wow he really was a sucker. I continued, 'I don't want any trouble. I just wanted to help that girl.'

'OK. You can stay one night.'

BINGO I had him!

'Thanks man, I really appreciate you helping me out. You really did save a life out there.' I said it deliberately to massage his ego (that always helps).

'We can start again... do the interview.'

'Do you think I could take a shower first? I had to hide out so, um, I need to freshen up.'

'Ah, sure, I guess that would be OK.'

He looked confused as though it might be a trick, but he led me down the hallway anyway.

I counted one closet and two bedrooms. It felt pretty risky, what I was about to do, but I decided that Samm and I would be out of there and on a bus to Brisbane before he'd have a chance to call the cops. He'd barely remember us in a week.

He showed me the bathroom and where the towels were. I closed the door behind him and turned on the taps, letting the water run warm. As I got undressed, I decided I wasn't going to wash my clothes in the shower this time. He'd think I was a weirdo or something. The truth is, I wanted a shower just as much as I wanted to raid his bathroom for stuff I could sell. If we were going to make a sell worthwhile, then I had to grab a few things that held some value. I opened the cupboards underneath the sink and sifted through while the running water masked any sound I made. I found an electric razor toward the back of the shelf and figured it probably never really got used anyway, so I hid it in my jacket.

I stepped into the shower and let the pitta patter of warm velvet drops roll off my body, washing the stench that was stuck to my skin far down the drain. It always amazed me how good it felt to have warm water running over your skin. Using my feet, I covered the hole leading to the pipes below, flooding the base of the shower. I wondered if all of my stored up tears, would fill that glassed shower box. If I ever let myself feel them, release them, cry them, would they swallow me up? I started to think about Lena, how small and cute she was. The guilt bubbled up inside me like boiling water in a kettle. The memory soon passed as another filled my brain... that day in the alley. Just flashes, no faces, but I remembered Jase's bright red and white new sneakers. At the moment of that memory, I heaved up in the shower. My stomach convulsed as though it had years of waste that needed to come out. My stomach was empty, so not one thing actually left my mouth. Once I got control of the heaving inside my body, I hoped that DB hadn't heard a thing (I really had to learn his name).

I got out of the shower and dressed quickly, not knowing exactly how long I had been in there. I didn't want him to get suspicious and call the cops.

As I grabbed my jacket and opened the bathroom door, he called out my name, 'Lisa?' Well not my real name.

I walked into the bedroom that was closest to the bathroom door. In there was DB, standing on a chair, pulling some garbage bags from out of the wardrobe.

'I found these last night,' he said, while pulling out another bag. 'No one bothered to clean out this place, just threw sheets on the furniture and left. Grans clothes were still hanging in the other wardrobe.'

He dropped another bag on the floor in front of me.

'I guess Gran never got round to dropping these off at church. She thought collecting for the less fortunate was Gods work. I was going to drop them at Vinnies, but if you want to have a look at them?'

Great! Even his gran was a do-gooder. Believing in God. Does nobody know he doesn't exist? I shook my head at DB, as if to say, 'whatever'. I doubted that there was anything good in those bags for me but I was silently hoping for a new T-shirt.

I sat on the end of the bed and placed my jacket carefully on the floor, making sure the razor didn't come flying out. As I opened one of the bags, I noticed DB was kind of staring at me. So I stared back at him.

'Ah, I'll leave you to it, to look… um I'll go review some questions… ah…' he stumbled, then he left the room.

So I sat there on my own and opened the first bag. I found a white dress, soft, silky to touch. It had pretty little pink flowers on it. Pretty. That word kind of made me laugh. I hadn't thought about nice dresses or nice things at all for a very long time.

I remember the day I first arrived in Sydney, after Daisy died. I saw those girls with their bouncy shiny hair, floating out of that gelato shop wearing really pretty dresses. They looked like some kind of rehearsed dance as they laughed and smiled at one another with their bags swinging over their shoulders. I wanted to be like them.

I took off my clothes and slid the dress on over my head. It drifted down my body with no effort at all. It felt like soapy water that was somehow dry on my skin. I looked up at myself in the mirror and saw myself smiling. I couldn't remember the last time I looked in a mirror. My hair was blonde and dreadlocked, it was like a ball of fur. I was clean. I showered well, but my eyes looked tired and worn and soon my smile faded as I realised, I would never be one of those girls. Too damaged, too broken, too ugly.

BANG BANG BANG, interrupted my thoughts. I walked over to the window and saw Sammy sitting outside in the backyard on this sort of couch swing thing.

Sammy! You are going to get us busted! I yelled inside my head. I couldn't believe Samm was so stupid… wait, what was I saying? Of course Samm was that stupid! He doesn't stop to think.

I threw my oversized T-shirt over the top of the dress and quietly opened the bedroom door. I peered around the corner and I could see DB sitting on the couch, laptop open and the TV on. I quietly turned left and tiptoed toward the backdoor, which was wide open. I was grateful that Sammy didn't just walk on inside. I was also grateful the fresh air was sweeping through the house, clearing out the mothball smell. I wasn't really sure why Ty called it mothball but I knew the smell (you know, like an Op Shop).

As I walked into the backyard, Sammy was grinning, arms up, wrapped around the back of his neck.

'Ahh this is the life hey Ange?' he said through a smile.

'You're going to get us busted!' I picked him up by the arm like a scolding mother and forcefully maneuvered him toward the bins where he was supposed to hide.

'But I'm hungry and bored. Come on Angie let me inside. At least get me something to eat?'

He really knows how to grate on my nerves. There was a time and place for joking and this wasn't it and nor was scaring me in that stupid dress! I left him down by the side of the bin and huffed back toward the door.

'Hey Angie,' he called out.

I turned back around.

'Nice legs,' he cheekily uttered, raising his eyebrows up and down. Then he ducked back down behind the bin. That little shi…

'You OK?'

I turned around and it was DB. Snap went the trap and I was back on.

'Oh yeah, fine. Just getting some fresh air but it's getting cold,' I said rubbing my arms and ushered us both toward the back door and away from Sammy!

'Um have you got something to eat?' I asked, following him back inside to the kitchen.

'I was going to make some cheese toasties. Not exactly gourmet, but ah…'

'It's food,' I responded.

'Right,' he agreed.

We walked into the kitchen and he grabbed some cheese and butter out of the fridge, which looked like a hundred years old (the fridge not the cheese or the butter). I got the feeling this was his grandma's house and she must have been like a hundred years old. So the fridge was really very fitting.

Cheese or butter? DB held out, indicating which job I was to do. I picked cheese. Love that shit.

'Cheese it is,' he said, handing me a knife and a chopping board. 'How many do you want?'

'Four.'

'Four?'

'Yeah four,' I repeated. Was he stupid? Although I guess the equation didn't really add up, unless you knew Sammy was outside. Still I'm a homeless chick. I'm hungry.

He turned on the grill by lighting a match and began to butter the bread.

He then asked me, 'I was thinking, perhaps you could help me fold some pamphlets tomorrow? I have a whole heap to get through and... well, if you help me, then we'll call it square.'

'You mean the three hundred bucks?' I asked as I handed him the slices of cheese that I sort of butchered. It's not like I sliced things all that often.

'Well two really. A hundred was to answer some questions.'

My immediate reaction was no. So I said, 'I don't know. I've got a lot of stuff I have to do tomorrow.' Which you and I know isn't true, but then I thought about it and realised if I did help him with whatever he was talking about, pamphlet things, then maybe we would be able to stay at his place for another night, which would give us more time. Sammy could set the ID thing up with one of the "bro's". He did say it might take a couple of days.

So I changed my mind and said, 'OK.'

'OK.' DB agreed, then he put the sandwiches in the grill and gave me a can of coke from out of the fridge. Sweet, sweet coke, bubbly, fizzy, zing! Like an explosion in my mouth.

'How long have you been on the streets?' he asked.

'A long time.' A really long lifetime. Felt like multiple lifetimes.

'Did you have a fight with your parents?'

'Something like that.' (You and I know better. It was horrific).

'It seems nonsensical to run away because of a fight.'

What a nard! 'Don't you think that maybe life on the streets is better than whatever shit house home you're coming from?' I said it with bitterness and anger. How could he not know that? Nonsensical, do you mean it doesn't make sense? English please!

'I guess I don't understand how it could be better?'

Annoys me when rich kids say stupid shit. No of course you don't realise because you lived in a house with a white picket fence and a dog and home made cookies, singing family songs around the piano, waxing your expensive car that mummy and daddy bought for you.

I finally responded with, 'no you wouldn't cause you're a rich boy.'

I got up off the stool and sat at the table. He pulled out the toasties and put them down in front of me. I ate the first one in about five seconds flat. The cheesy deliciousness coated my teeth and caressed my belly, soothing my hunger pains before dissolving them altogether.

'I guess I deserved that,' DB finally said. I think he felt stupid.

I don't know why I said this, 'I barely remember it.' Maybe it's cause I didn't... but then I had never tried to either.

'What do you remember?' he asked.

As I took a breath in, I stopped. I actually tried to remember. 'Mum going crazy. One time she locked me inside her friend's house. I tried to run out but her friend barricaded the door.' I then paused, lost in that moment that had clearly scarred me. 'I don't know...' I was annoyed at myself for saying it. 'As soon as I got a chance to run, I ran.'

I hadn't thought about that night in forever, not even sure why I told him. I had spoken not one single word about my past, about my home, before the streets to anyone. Not Sammy, not Ty, not even Daisy. No one asked and I never told. Sydney town was clearly screwing with my brain, as was this guy. It was like, ask a question and I will spill the beans... but why now?

Then he asked me, 'what about your Dad?'

'I'm pretty tired,' was all that I said. I was back in control. I picked up my plate and walked to the bedroom as though the conversation never happened and as though he never asked that question. What question? Exactly. No question.

I waited until it was dark outside to open the bedroom window.

'Samm,' I whispered out.

No reply.

'Samm,' I called out again a little louder. Still nothing.

'Sammy!' I almost said at full vocal level.

Then I saw Sammy's crusty little face pop up from behind the bin. He had fallen asleep.

'Take long nough?' he said as he climbed in through the window. His crustiness soon faded when I passed him two cheesy toasties. It was like his birthday had come and I had bought him a pony! Ahhh the simple things. Didn't take much to make us happy.

Samm sat up on the bed against the wall and scoffed down his food. I curled up next to him and told him, 'plans have changed slightly. I reckon I can get us to stay here tomorrow night… if I didn't just mess it up.' I said that last bit almost under my breath.

'What ya mean?' Samm asked with a mouthful of food.

'Gives me time to grab more stuff, maybe cash too, plus you got to locate your bro's.' I said bro's while bending my pointy and middle finger on both of my hands, emphasizing his so called "bro's".

Samm kept munching away with his mouth full of cheese and toast, 'nah I know where they are, Ace is staying at Brado's on Vic Street.'

'Who's Ace?'

'Me bro!'

I could feel my eyes getting heavy and was losing the struggle to fight the sleepiness and Sammy, about the so-called bro's. He once told me that all aboriginals are bro's (brothers) that they always find each other and they always help each other out. It was kind of nice really. I wondered why the rest of us didn't feel that way too? Too scared to trust what the other one might do to us, whereas with Samm and his bro's, they knew they were safe together. Seemed pretty foreign to me. I never really felt welcome when he grouped together with them. It hadn't happened all that often, but still I always felt like they were eye-balling me or something. Actually I felt that way with just about everyone. I was always on guard in case the next person attacked me.

'Who can offload?' I asked through droopy eyes, getting comfy next to Samm.

'They got people. It'll be cool. They got a job for me hey, smash and grab.'

My skin tried to jump off my bones in order to show what a big NO I wanted to say, but the sleepiness held it down, I barely flinched at all.

'We'll do it this way first... just get a contact, come back here,' I drowsily said.

'Nah, I'll stay with me bro's. I'm not sitting out there again.'

Not another word left my lips, as I fell asleep quicker than I ever remember falling asleep before.

CHAPTER THIRTY THREE

AND SO IT BEGINS

I woke up in a panic. Samm was asleep beside me while DB knocked on the door.

'Lisa, you awake?'

'Um, I'm just getting dressed. Don't come in!' I yelled out nervous as hell. 'Samm you gotta get up!'

I shook him as quietly as I could.

'You okay?' DB called out again.

'Yep, fine!' I shouted back.

Samm rubbed his eyes and groaned, 'what's going on?'

I opened the window and pulled Samm to it. 'Time to go. Pawn that ring, then come back.'

'I'm staying with me bro's,' he told me as he jumped out the window.

'They're not your bro's!' I barked back under silent breath. Actually it was more of a silent meow than a bark.

'We look after each other, bro's!' he exclaimed with animated arms, bouncing his hands from off his chest.

It was neither the place nor the time to be arguing with him, but I had to state my case.

'If Jase sees you… we shouldn't split up.'

I tried to convince him, but really it was no use. I knew he was going to do whatever he wanted to do and when he cheekily chimed back at me, 'no worries LISA!' I knew I had lost the battle. That damn name!

'Fine! Come back here tomorrow,' I ordered.

'Call me,' Samm sang out while moonwalking across the backyard. 'Brado's, Vic Street. Google that shit!' And with that he did a little tap dance and climbed the back fence.

For someone with barely an education at all, he was pretty smart. I guess I'd have to Google that shit later.

'Be careful,' I hushed out as I pulled my head inside the window, then popped it straight back out as I remembered what he said to me the night before, 'no smash and grabs!'

I'm sure he was 'yeah yeah yeahing' me, as I shut the window.

I waited for some time to pass before I walked out of the room and into the kitchen. I thought maybe I should ask DB what his real name was, but decided the time had well and truly passed into complete awkwardness where I actually couldn't ask him anymore. Time started to feel weird to me. His name was Douchebag, mine was Lisa and Sammy was out hanging with his bro's. What the hell was going on!

'OJ?' DB asked me as he stood at the kitchen bench pouring a glass for himself.

I nodded my head 'yes' as I walked toward the kitchen table. It reminded me of when Ty would give me OJ in the morning. TY! I had completely forgotten about Ty! I had to contact him immediately! I rummaged my hand through my pocket and felt the piece of paper with his number on it, scrunched up in a tiny ball.

'Did you sleep OK?' DB asked.

'Yep,' I said, darting my eyes across the room in search of a phone. BINGO! Corner table, by the doorway leading out of the kitchen. I was going to need some serious slight of hand. So I took the opportunity as DB reached for another glass, turning away from me. I swiped the phone and hurriedly headed for the bathroom before DB had a chance to notice I was gone. As I closed the door behind me, I wished for no lock on the phone and as luck would have it, the fool was more trusting than I originally imagined. No lock! I typed as quickly as I could: BRADOS ON VIC STREET - GOOGLE THAT SHIT and then chuckled to myself as I imagined Sammy moonwalking across the backyard. I then typed into the phone, SAFE. WILL HEAD NORTH 2 OR 3 DAYS. DON'T REPLY! I typed in the number Ty had given me and as soon as I sent it, I deleted it. Mission accomplished!

I stepped silently out from the bathroom and headed down the hallway, peering my head around the corner. I could see DB on his laptop in the front room with two glasses of OJ sitting on the table. I put the phone back on the shelf by the kitchen door and turned quietly toward his bedroom. I was taking the opportunity to grab something that could be of value.

Once I was inside DB's bedroom, I caught a floorboard under my foot that wanted to squeak. I held my breath and went red for a couple of seconds (which felt like hours), waiting to see if he had heard me or not. But I heard nothing. No footsteps drew near, so I reached out for the wardrobe door and took a hold of the handle. I squeezed it so tight, as though by doing so it wouldn't make a noise. Ha! It creaked louder than the floorboard squeaked! It sent a bit of panic in my chest. I could feel the pulsating panic flowing up into my brain and thump like a swollen drum inside my ear. It was the sound of the beat from a guilty, fearful heart. I wasn't so sure I still had one (a heart that is).

No one came. No one heard, so I continued my raid and approached the bedside table, opening the draw to find socks and undies. The place was basically empty. I started to realise that the whole plan to sell a bunch of stuff was out the window. He had nothing. The only way we would make some mula, would be to swipe his wallet. If it held some cash or a credit card, then I could take it and head straight out the door, find Sammy and get out of dodge (Sydney), otherwise we were going to walk away empty-handed and I couldn't have that. I wasn't really sure why I hadn't just done that to begin with (steal his credit card). Idiot! One too many knocks to the head I suppose.

I disappointedly crept back out into the hallway and stopped for a moment, composing myself and settling my breath after the burst of adrenaline from the squeaky creaky room.

I walked into the front room and DB was still sitting on the couch. As I approached, he turned around and smiled at me. He closed his laptop and stood up, opening a box by the side of the couch. He began to pull out some glossy coloured paper.

'We should start folding,' he said with warmth, continuing to smile, placing piles of paper on top of the glass table. 'I'll do these ones, you do those.'

I sat down on the armchair as he passed me a pile. I wondered why he was still being nice to me? He didn't seem repulsed, he wasn't trying to shoo me out the door; he was just nice. I had to remind myself to stop thinking like that, otherwise it would be harder to take the wallet and run. It was already difficult cause his face reminded me so much of Daisy. She was kind to me too. I think it was his smile, it was just like hers, the kind that lights up a room, makes you wanna hang out, not trying to be anything... just being. Feels good, I guess is what I'm trying to say. I always felt good around Daisy. We would talk for hours. I don't remember what about, just stuff. Nothing serious, just random whatever. We laughed a lot. She was amazing.

I folded the first sheet of glossy paper and asked, 'who's this?' I was referring to a guy with a massive fake smile, printed on the front cover. He had big white teeth, dressed in a suit. Looked like one of those dudes you see on those massive For Sale signs, out the front of houses.

'My brother, Damian. He will be running for a seat in the Senate.'

'What?' I had no idea what he was talking about.

'Government. Most people find it boring. It's part of fundraising for pre-selection. Got to bring in the dollars.' He said it like I was supposed to know what that meant, then he continued, 'I'm not so sure Australia can handle his ego.' That part he said with distaste, like he didn't really like the guy.

I never had a brother or a sister so I don't know what it's like, but if I did have a brother, I hoped he'd look after me like Jase looked after Lena... although look at how that turned out.

'Why you doing it?' I asked.

'Rent.'

I figured maybe this was his brother's house after all. Maybe his gran gave it to him or something. DB looked pretty shitty about folding the flyer things, but look at the place... pretty sweet if you ask me. Who cares if you have to fold some paper for locks on the door, a hot shower, plenty of food... didn't seem so bad. It smelt old, but it was in pretty good nick. The smell was more stuffy than old anyway, like a window needed to be cracked. We never had that problem in a squat. Windows were always cracked and broken or not there at all, but still, for some reason they always stunk like piss.

It then clicked in my head that the For Sale sign guy, on the front of the pamphlet, was the tall dude from the other day. The one that was standing by the front door staring at me and blocking my escape. The pompous looking dude.

'You don't look alike,' I said.

'Butchers son,' DB replied. It was as though he could read my mind that I didn't really get what he was saying cause he added, 'it's an old saying... never mind. Do you have a brother or sister?'

'Nope.'

'Are you on your own out there?'

'No one stays alone. Too dangerous. Safety in numbers.'

'So you're not on your own?'

'I have Sammy.'

'Boyfriend?'

Now that made me laugh!

'No!' I said between laughter. Ah Sammy... boyfriend!

'Where is he?'

'With friends.'

'Did you grow up in a housing estate?'

I sniggered at that question before I answered it.

'why does everyone think that!' I said it as a state-ment and not a question. 'You don't think you can come from money and have fucked up parents?'

'I know you can have messed up parents but wouldn't someone notice if kids were being neglect-ed? Wouldn't child protection step in?'

I sniggered to myself again. Actually it was more of a massive sigh relieving the humour in it.

'Yeah, we had them come through once. Great job they did.'

They were shit! Came through once! Once! In all those years with everything she did and then I lied because I was so shit scared of what she would do to me and it was like they knew, like they couldn't be bothered, like they ticked me off a list and then went out for coffee. Fuck I hated coffee. The breath of my mother stunk like stinky coffee. I'd die before I drank that shit and then spat that foul smell all over some-one else's face while I was talking to them.

'I thought you were all on drugs and that's why you end up on the streets.'

'They are on drugs,' I said honestly. 'How else do you survive the shit we do? All we are seen as is drug-gie's and criminals... we're trying to survive.'

'People should know the real story. If our system doesn't work, then policy needs to change.'

He was starting to piss me off. I had no idea what policy was or what he was going on about. I could feel my neck beginning to swell with frustration and the anger heating up my skin. He was butterflying into a do-gooder right in front of me, out to change the world and annoying the hell out of me! He didn't know jack shit about what goes on and how little people care, how we basically mean shit to anyone in this society.

'Nobody cares,' I responded, still folding the pamphlets, trying to keep my cool.

He continued on about the Government and something something. What I heard was this; policy, blah blah blah blah blah. Public Support, blah blah blah, law. So I responded accordingly with, 'whatever.' But that didn't shut him up!

He continued, 'people have to know about it, to care about it.'

'People ain't never gonna care about us,' I blurted back.

'They will if they know the truth. Don't you think people should know the truth?'

'No.' I said it cause I already knew the answer. No one cared about us.

'We could write the real story. You could tell me about how people live on the streets, their background. I can pick the facts that tie into my research, give another perspective?'

Another perspective? What the hell sort of article was this anonymous do-gooder trying to write? A Sunday paper sob story? A guilt trip sparking the idea that something needs to be done, only for every reader to turn to the next page and forget about us? What's the point! What's the point in feeling it in the first place if you don't do anything about it? I don't know what he was expecting from me, but there was no way I could possibly drag it all up, combust from the inside out from everything I had seen, then wrap it up into a little parcel and present it to his smiling face.

'No!' I said to him again.

'It's your chance to have a say.'

Oh my god I wanted to scream at him. 'I said no!'

I didn't wait for another "let's change the world speech" one friggin insignificant article at a time. I got up and walked out. I walked straight out of the house, into the backyard and huffed myself onto a seat. I wasn't sure at the time why I chose that couch swing to sit on but it was starting to feel like a corny movie, storming out like a sulking wife and sitting in that chair. Maybe that's what I liked about being at that house, the fact that it almost felt like my life could turn out like a movie.

DB followed me outside to the chair. I looked at him with my arms folded shut across my chest as he sat down beside me.

'Why do you care?' I asked, looking at him puzzled and annoyed.

'I didn't. But it sounds like a voice needs to be heard. It's part of my job... well hopefully will be my job. I can't guarantee that it will get published...'

'So then what's the point?' I asked confused.

'I think we can put something powerful together. The relevance to this year's budget will be the deciding factor for publication. I can make it work.'

What he meant by budget, I wasn't sure. I wasn't going to do it. What would be the point? I wouldn't do him no favours, no matter how much he looked like Daisy. I was going to take his wallet remember!

Then he said, 'I'll split the fee with you.'

Ahh that magic word, mula. Money was what I needed, but what was he getting out of it? If there was one thing I had learnt, it was nothing came to me for free or just to help me out.

'What do you get out of it?'

'A job. Never go back to Canberra.'

'So you're not a journo then? You don't even live here?' I rolled my eyes as I said it cause it appeared to be empty promises again.

'This is my grans house, was my grans house. I need this article to get the job.'

I could see he had no real interest in helping me out. It was all for a job. See what I was saying, nothing for nothing.

'What about that girl the other day?' he asked, trying to get me to care.

'Who? Lizzy?' I didn't even know the girl, but he didn't know that.

'You helped her... this could help others.'

Helping other girls like me was something I wanted to do before Ty went to jail, but that was a long time ago. Things had changed. I felt like everything he was saying was all wish-wash. I didn't need to help people. I needed money, money to go north and that's it.

'I need five hundred bucks,' I finally said.

'That's a high number,' he replied.

'I provide the content. You get a job. Seems fair to me.'

He must have wanted that job pretty bad cause all he said was, 'you've got yourself a deal.'

CHAPTER THIRTY FOUR

SPILL YA GUTS

I agreed. Can you believe that I agreed? I felt unsure, like I was moving into something that I wasn't prepared for. Was I over dramatizing it? Maybe. When DB started to ask me questions to get the flow going, I felt uncomfortable. I'm not sure if he realised how I was feeling, but he gave me a few minutes to myself while he went back inside to grab his laptop, the one I almost stole. Ha! If I had of, I wouldn't even be in this situation facing a gazillion questions. But, I told myself to get over it. I had five hundred bucks coming my way and I was OK with that (the money).

As I sat uncomfortably twirling my thumbs on that couch swing out back, I looked out at the trees that lined the back fence and began to wonder where each one came from. I found myself silently asking when were they planted and how they grew? I answered the questions to myself, realising it didn't really matter who planted the seed or who bought the seed, the seed was planted and the trees grew. It didn't matter when it happened, how it happened, if it was one person or twenty people that did it. What mattered was they grew. I decided that it was true for me too. You see, it was far easier to look back, backwards into those years gone by and see multiple girls, not me, but me. I'm not making any sense am I? What I mean is, to re-tell those stories, to answer the kind of questions DB was asking me, it didn't have to be me. I didn't have to act like they were me, say they were me or even be me at all. It didn't matter who they happened to, it just mattered that they happened.

'Hey Lisa, would you like a drink?' DB called out from the back door.

'Sure,' I called back.

'Coke OK?'

'Yep,' was my response.

I didn't want to seem too eager, but really I was dancing on the inside. Sweet sweet coke again. I smiled to myself thinking, I really could get used to this lifestyle.

Looking back, there was more to me staying there than just the money. I felt safe.

'Thanks,' I said, reaching for the can of coke DB was holding out for me.

'Sure, no worries.' Then he gave me the twinkle. Remember that smile Daisy used to give me? It was the same one.

I couldn't shake the comment that he made earlier about the job, about not being a journo. I didn't get how this was all coming together, the article, the money. To be honest, I wanted to make sure the five hundred bucks was definitely coming my way.

'What did you mean when you said, "hopefully it will be my job"?'

He took a deep sigh in (not out as expected). Not even sure how you sigh in, but that's what he did. It was more of a weighted heavy breath. By the sound of it, I knew there was a long story behind it, but I wasn't sure if he was going tell me all the details or not. I was kind of hoping he didn't. I don't like personal stories, especially if the person telling the story is sad. I don't feel, remember? (No heart). I don't feel and I don't want to start.

'I'm competing with five other people for one role at the Journal. It's a financial/political magazine; rivals the Financial. It's a little more juicy, it's... it's what I want to do... write.'

The confused look on my face must have said I don't follow, cause he continued, 'I've been groomed for politics.' As he said it, the frown in-between his eyebrows increased but so did his smile, like a love hate relationship. Like when it's real cold and you get undressed and your face gets all wrinkled up, but you jump in a hot shower and smile at the warmth.

'Six years of study, six years of University newspapers, silently writing for a way out, away from politics.'

I think that last part was an attempt at humour ("writing" instead of "hoping"), but I didn't flinch.

Kind of like what I do to Samm by not laughing. If he thought I thought it was funny, then he would think we were friends and we weren't.

DB continued in the same way Sammy would have, smiling like he almost knew my game (but I'm sure they both didn't).

'My thesis won some awards. I caught the eye of the Journal who requested I apply for an internship and here I am, down to the last six applicants. This article is important to me as well as to you.'

'I never said it was important to me. As long as you pay me the five hundred bucks then, then...'

'Aha,' he laughed out, 'I'll pay you your five hundred bucks.'

It sounded like it was the first time he had ever used the word "bucks" with his rounded perfect manicured English. With all that private school education, seemed stupid he needed me to get some job hey?

DB's smile faded and he showed little emotion to the next words he said, 'if the article doesn't cut it, then back to my Masters and politics.'

'Why do something you don't want, when you want to do something else? Seems stupid to me,' I said it in my most ocker, drawn out broad Aussie accent I could muster.

DB's face lifted, as did the corner of his lips. He looked at me and asked, 'you have never done something that you would rather not do because of someone else?'

OK he had a point and he knew it.

'I don't know... maybe,' I said, but of course I had. Like Ty did for me, I did for Sammy. I guess we all did shit we hate to look after someone else. But this dude had a choice; this isn't life or death stuff for him. He could have done whatever he wanted.

As though reading my mind again he said, 'sounds stupid still? Maybe it is. I guess when you are the son of my father, you feel like some things you have to do.'

'What's so special about him?'

'My father is the Australian Treasurer.'

'The what?'

He laughed at me! Well not laughed exactly, but one of those cheeky endearing smiles with the slight sound of breath. It was annoying because it was cute (can't believe I just said that... cute!), but he was laughing at me!

'Why are you laughing at me?' The lines in my frown deepened as his smile widened!

'Not at you,' he said and then let out more of that lightened laughed breath. 'It's my father, he loves his own importance. The fact that you don't know who he is, he'd say that's why you're homeless. It's more ignorant than you having no idea who he is. That's why. It wasn't you,' he smiled wider (and I hate to admit it), but he was twinkling the shit out of his eyes (as in Daisy's twinkle x 100!). 'Not everyone's laughing at you,' he disclosed with warmth in his voice.

His smiled stayed, dimples like pinholes and my lips tilted up. Yes! I smiled. As soon as I realised I was doing it, I shook my head and shook away that stupid fluffy weirdness I was feeling and lightness and whatever cute... what? I was lost for words. I lost my words and forgot where I was in the conversation.

'What was the question?' I asked, indicating toward his laptop, which he began to open while STILL SMILING. I bit the inside of my lip and looked toward the back door as though wanting to escape, while DB looked at the laptop screen.

It was quiet and yet my head was full.

I started with the small stuff. Breaking into houses, the camp by the willow, a squatter's house for ten. The more I talked, the wind seemed to intensify, so we moved inside to the kitchen. I sat myself on top of the bench still looking out toward the trees, holding sight of them, keeping them in my view, reminding myself that it wasn't important who was in the stories, just that the stories themselves were important, to continue pretending that they weren't about me.

As the day moved forward more information was divulged. The story of Daisy told as a secondary listener, as though a girl like Lizzy crossed me in the streets and spoke of this almost fanciful occurrence of a deep nightmare. As I finished that story, DB handed me a mug with warm milk and honey. Can you believe it! Like the ones I often thought of being handed by a curly headed mother when I was just twelve; it's what I dreamt of for years on the streets. This guy was handing me that very same cup I envisioned, to calm my nerves, to soothe the pain, for he was feeling what I had seen, what he thought I had heard… but you and I know that those things were really me, through my eyes. They happened to me.

As darkness fell, it was like once the door was open, I couldn't push it shut and although I never once put myself in any of the scenarios that I told him, I did tell him about Hoe, which was really Pho. I thought it best to change his name (just in case)… but I told him.

Words kept pouring out of my mouth like a water pipe at the end of a storm. There was no containing it and there was no going back. I had bared my soul to this stranger, this guy who I hadn't even asked for his name, who didn't even know my real name. I talked of myself as though I was somebody else, talking of a girl I once knew, which was kind of true. The girl in the field that first day, the girl that was in Sydney all alone and the girl that once felt so safe inside Ty's arms, but she wasn't me, she was somebody else. Some long distant past that I could only remember in flashes, like woven dreams in the morning, strung together through blocks of time, never really knowing the whole story, just remembering the flashes. I was remembering the flashes and giving them up to DB, to do what with? I didn't really know, but something in me felt lighter, something in me almost burned, but not in a bad "I'm cn fire" sort of way, in a way that felt almost like... I didn't really know, but it was almost as though I was starting to feel alive.

CHAPTER THIRTY FIVE

ALIVE
WHERE'S SAMMY

I woke up the next day and wow! I had never slept like that before. It was deep, as if I had nothing to worry about, no guard to put up, no guard to be on… and so I slept. As I rolled over to hit Sammy's arm, I realised where I was and suddenly jumped up. I must have fallen asleep on the couch at DB's house. I didn't remember falling asleep. I was warm, a pillow under my head. DB must have put it there. I think my heart moved, like a small moment of realisation or questioning; would someone care for me enough to place a pillow under my head? Without trying to take something? Without trying to hurt me?

ANGE! SAMMY! I shrieked at myself! and snapped to attention and out of my head. I had to call Sammy!

I almost tripped over my own feet as I rushed to-ward the kitchen. I could hear DB on the phone, yell-ing at someone. I needed to use his phone! As I turned the corner, almost tripping over my own foot again, DB slammed his phone down on the bench. Please don't be broken! I cried out within myself, unconcerned with what had happened between him and the other person on the phone.

'Can I use your phone?' I asked.

He took a while to compute what I had said, as the redness in his face began to settle.

'Um sure,' finally came out of his mouth hesitantly, as he looked from his phone to me, then back to the phone again.

I took the phone and stared at him in an awkward silence. I felt like saying, do you want to watch me make the call or can the big girl dial it herself? But before it left my mouth he said, 'right' and left the room.

'Google that shit,' I said under my breath. Sure Sammy, I'll Google that shit.

I searched for Brado's hostel phone number in KX (Kings Cross) and dialed.

'Hi.' I said to some guy on the other end of the phone. 'Is Sammy there?'

As the dude cn the other end of the phone told me to hold on, I suddenly felt really guilty about DB's gold ring and the razor. Shit! The razor!

I rushed to the bedroom and searched through the pile of clothes on the floor. Ah 'YES!' I found it!

'Yeah,' said the voice on the other end of the phone.

'Samm?'

'Who's this?'

He was pissed off with me. I could tell.

'Don't play around,' I said.

'I'm not. Don't know no one called Ange.'

'I never said my name. I've got good news!'

'Ya better after ditching me.'

And there it was. I knew it. I knew that he was pissed with me. We've come so far together and he acts all tough and big and brave but really he can't be without me. I felt like neither of us could be without each other. It felt weird when we were apart.

'I'll meet you at Brougham Lane OK?' It was the only place I could think of, the safe spot. I didn't want to meet him on Victoria Street where Brado's was. Number one, I wasn't there to make friends, I wasn't going to meet the "bro's" (they'd hate me anyway, white chick with big dreads), plus (and more importantly) I didn't want to bump into Jase. He was still out there, he knew I was in Sydney and I didn't want to waltz on down Victoria Street like a big red beacon to his gang, whoever they might be. This way I could sneak up into the laneway, meet Samm and sort out our tickets to Brissy.

Samm finally agreed and I hung up the phone. As I did, I looked at the razor and it clicked in my head, I had to get that ring back. After everything, I felt like I couldn't take it away from DB. Samm and I would have our five hundred bucks, so we didn't need his ring. That was enough to get us out of Sydney, away from Jase and far away from Pho.

I quietly walked into the bathroom and opened the cabinet door with such care, so that it didn't squeak and lightly placed the razor on the shelf toward the back.

When I walked back into the hall, DB was sitting in the front room typing on his laptop. I walked up and said, 'I kind of need a favor.'

'OK?'

'That was a lot of information... about all those girls.'

'It was,' DB said, getting up from off his chair. 'I chose the most relevant to link with. I think I nailed it.'

'Maybe you could give me some of that money? I have to meet Samm. It's for him.'

'You know you never talked about Sammy.'

'Nothing to say.'

To me Samm was off limits, I didn't talk about him.

DB contemplated my request for a few seconds, then nodded his head as though he thought it through and decided it was fair.

'I'll come with you, stop by the ATM.'

I let a deep breath out, not realising that I had been holding it in. I think I was afraid to ask the question. I wanted the money, actually I needed the money so Samm could go down to the bus station and put two tickets on hold to Brisbane. I didn't know if they needed cash for that but just in case they did, I wanted him to take some.

DB didn't live too far from KX, from the laneway. We walked in silence for a while and I wondered if he was exhausted by me or repelled by me after what I told him. I hadn't seen the twinkle again and... well... I kind of missed it. It wasn't as though he seemed disgusted by me or anything, it's just that I was so used to people not wanting to be around me that it kind of made me feel awkward that he didn't mind being around me. I knew he was hanging around because he wanted my stories, but I don't know... it just felt like he didn't mind it either. We were in a way doing a favour for each other, me getting to Brisbane and him getting that job. It felt good.

'What happened to Samm?' he asked me again.

Here we go I thought to myself. Didn't I make it clear that Samm is off limits?

'What? Nothing,' I said.

'Why is he on the streets?'

'Why do you want this job so bad?'

Two can play that game of what neither one of us wants to talk about. I mean, really, it was just a job. He could get another.

More awkward silence passed.

'Do you ever feel like you don't belong?' DB asked me.

I stopped and looked at him like YOU'RE AN IDIOT!

'Ah yep right,' he said feeling a bit sheepish. 'I got forced into politics. My brother, as you know is also in politics. Damian can do no wrong but I've always been the screw up, not a typical Burgess. My mother is drunk more than she is sober and I wonder who my father hates more, me or my mother?'

He stopped and looked up at me and asked, 'can you hear the violins playing?'

We both laughed. It was pretty funny.

He continued, still smiling, 'no seriously, my father hates journalists and the fact that I bailed on my Masters. The last thing I want to do is return to Canberra.'

DB's smile was warm and soft. It made me smile when he smiled and if there's one thing I know about, it's hate and dads.

'His mum died of cancer.'

'Sammy's?'

I nodded yes and then he asked, 'what about his Dad?'

We had arrived at the ATM and I continued to tell him what happened as DB withdrew the money.

'Lost his job, stopped talking, eating, then child services took Samm away. He killed himself after that.'

My heart sank further as I felt sorrow for Sammy. I wanted to see him right in that very moment and throw my arms around him. Let him know that it was him that mattered most to me.

More awkward silence passed.

It was like awkward gift cards were being given out that day and I was receiving every one of them.

'I'll catch up with ya, in ten OK?'

I said it without waiting for DB's response, as I was already heading off toward the laneway.

As I reached the other side of the road, Samm was sitting against the wall. I ran up and threw my arms around him.

'Jesus A, knock me out or som'em!' Samm exclaimed, pushing me off him.

'You K?' I asked.

'I'm fine. I can look after me self.'

I could see that he was still pissed with me so I ruffled his hair.

'Get off it A,' he said throwing my arm away.

'I got it!' I told him with delight!

Sammy stood up, 'got what?'

'Well I haven't got it just yet, not all of it, but five hundred smackaroos!'

'Yeah I believe when I see it. Have you got the cash?' He said it, not as a real question, but to make a point. 'Nah that's right, he hasn't even given it to you yet.'

'But he will, it's this article he has written and he'll get it, he'll give it to me.'

Samm was not convinced.

'Five hundred bucks Samm!' I repeated again.

'Ya trust him? Don't let him fill ya head with all that rich fella bullshit. Trust no one, stick together and we'll be alright, remember?'

'I also remember promising we'd never sleep in a bin or park ever again. We've got our money. We'll head north in two days. Here…' I shoved the hundred bucks in Sammy's hand. 'Put two tickets on hold.'

'You gonna stay there again?'

'I've got something else, these pamphlet's… don't worry, just come up when ya got the tickets sorted.'

'Nah Ange. I'll hang with my kind, you stick with yours.'

'It's like that is it?'

'Just do what cha gotta do.' Samm said in a sniggering sulk. Then he looked me up and down and mocked me. 'What's with the top A? You look stupid.'

I looked down and he was right. I was wearing a florally top I got out of one of the clothes bags DB left on the bedroom floor, the "grans" pile for Vinnies. It was fresh and clean. I felt new in it (as dumb as that may sound). I felt like I kind of blended in with everyone else, like I was part of the normal crowd.

'Shut up!' I snapped back at Samm.

'You all clean and shit. Bout time. I had to hold me breath every time you near, ay?'

Cheeky little fuc… 'I gotta go,' I said.

I turned to head off back toward DB when Samm yelled out, 'hey Ange, what else ya get?'

'What?' I replied almost confused.

'Jewelry? The laptop. Stuff we can sell?'

The thought of ripping DB off now made me feel sick in the stomach. It was like I totally forgot the plan. It had vanished from my mind, to rip this poor guy off.

'Samm, the ring. You sold his gold ring?'

'Certainly did,' he said with a smile.

'Shit,' I huffed from under my breath.

'How bout ya grab a bag, pack it, leave it out da front and I'll pick it up. Sell whatever's in it and we'll have more money when we head north.'

'Samm I need you to get that ring back.'

Samm just shook his head no.

'This guy is helping us. We've got the money, we'll have the money!'

'Until he decides to dump ya. He'll just use ya. They all use ya Angie.'

'Listen to me. You need to get that ring back.'

'Nah A, not doing it.' He said it defiantly.

I could see DB across the road and didn't want him to come over. I'm pretty sure Sammy would have gone all kung fu on his arse and I reckon he would have spilt the beans on the ring like it was some kind of one up on the imaginary scoreboard.

'I've got to go. Just get it back.'

By the half arsed smile he gave me and the way he kicked a stone on the ground, I knew I had him! Ha! I smiled, knowing that he would get that ring back.

As I headed off across the street, I turned back and yelled out, 'love you sweetie. See you later sugar pea,' and blew Samm a kiss. He threw his hand up at me and walked off in the other direction, down the laneway.

I turned back toward the road and giggled to myself. I don't know why I did? I guess it was at the thought of calling Samm sugar pea and sweetie. As my foot hit the curb on the other side of the road, I looked up and in front of me there were three girls stepping out of a shop and onto the pavement. It reminded me of those girls outside the gelato shop on the very first day I arrived in Sydney, all those years ago. Their dresses doing a dance as the wind blew through them. I could almost smell the freshness of their hair as the strands reflected perfect sunlight. Reality sunk in almost immediately, as I realised I would never be one of those girls.

'BOO!' DB jumped in front of me, literally scaring the pants off of me. What a dumb saying that was. My pants were clearly on and going nowhere fast.

'You were off in la la land,' he said.

I half smiled, watching the girls walk away. Then something weird happened, DB put his arm across my shoulder.

'Well forget la la land, we are off to a party! A boring occasion starring my brother, however it is free booze.'

'I'm not going,' I replied,

I was more focused on his arm that was around me than anything else. It was comforting, yet strange. Did it mean something? Was he being comforting? Did he notice me staring at those girls? Could he see what I was thinking? Of course not Ange! I told myself. Don't be so friggin stupid!

'We won't stay long. Drop some pamphlets off, ruffle some feathers, did I mention the free booze?'

He took his hand off my shoulder and waved down a taxi. We got inside the cab and he said to me, 'sorry we're kind of in a hurry, with everything that's happened, I forgot it was tonight.'

I shrugged my shoulders as though I didn't care. What I did care about was that his arm was off from around my shoulder. I wondered how I could think that? Why I thought that? Why I wanted his arm around my shoulder? It was all too weird, so I stared out the window the whole way back to his house.

CHAPTER THIRTY SIX

CINDERELLA
AT THE BALL

So it got weirder and more uncomfortable before it got better. In fact it didn't get any better, just more awkward. We came home... ha! I just said home. It wasn't my home, I meant his house. Anyway! We got back to his house, DB's. It was beginning to seem really not appropriate to be calling him DB (which was short for douchebag), when he was in actual fact really nice to me. He treated me like Samm did, like Ty did, like Daisy and Lucy did, like I was no different to him, that we were just two people hanging out, that we were the same. I wasn't annoying him nor was I in the way or disgusting, dirty or scary. He treated me like a real person.

We rushed through the last of the folding, preparing for his brothers event. I felt nervous and wondered why I even cared? DB got embarrassed when he suggested I wear a dress, the one with the pink flowers. Remember the one I tried on when Samm was waiting at the back door way too early? I didn't even realise he had seen it. He must have noticed it under my T-shirt (which made me more embarrassed) cause he said to me, 'you can put that on if you want, but it doesn't matter you can wear that too,' gesturing to what I was wearing (my dirty jeans and the floral top). I looked down at the ripped and tattered material of my jeans, I didn't really want to wear them, but could I actually wear a dress? As I thought about it, I bit the inside of my lip. It was a bad habit of mine, something I did when I was thinking about something important, but how could this be important to me? I mean, all I was doing was helping with some pamphlets and I didn't know anyone there and I didn't even know his real name. OH MY GOD! What was going on with me? Can you hear how I was ranting! I had to stop and breathe.

And that's what I did. I breathed. I went and had a shower. I pulled my hair back from off my face and kind of twisted it into a plait. It wasn't like amazing or anything, but it kind of looked nice compared to its normal pile of dreaded mess that sat on top of my head.

I walked into the bedroom and slipped on the dress. That silky feeling pressed against my skin; I felt different, not like me at all. Still, I didn't look in the mirror. I didn't want to see. I just wanted to go.

I walked out into the lounge as DB was tucking in his shirt. He was dressed like a gentleman. Does that make sense? Clothes that looked like silky water, sitting perfectly, charmingly, making him seem so… light.

He stopped fixing his shirt and stared at me, stuttering out, 'you, you…' and not saying anything more.

Oh God I thought to myself. I look like an idiot!

'I'll take it off.'

I went to leave the room when DB spat out, 'NO. I mean, no, don't, you look nice. It looks nice, the dress.'

Well that was even more awkward. Like I said, gift cards, loads of them full of awkwardness just for me. I lowered my head trying to cover my hot cheeks.

DB cracked the silence, clearing his throat and said, 'let's go.'

We each grabbed a box full of pamphlets and headed out the door. Not exactly Cinderella style, but instead of the pumpkin that turned into the carriage, I was the pumpkin that turned into a girl.

When we arrived at the fundraiser, DB carried both boxes up toward the front of the hotel. Lights were shining like beams crossing over one another. A long red carpet lay across the ground, acting as a pathway to the doors, inviting everyone in. Ahead of us more girls in dresses, each different, sparkling a different colour, doing a different kind of dance and in many different lengths. Some hanging heavy toward their ankles, while others were so short I'm sure I saw nickers! I stood frozen, asking myself, am I supposed to be here? I don't belong here! What am I...

'Lisa, Lisa?' DB said breaking my thoughts. 'Are you OK?'

He brought me back into that spot outside of the hotel and out of my head. I looked down at my feet noticing my own dress flowing through the breeze, jumping off my knees as though it was doing it's own little dance. A dress! I thought. Me, in a dress and it was dancing!

I looked up at DB and said, 'fine.'

We walked through the lobby and I was sure people were staring at me. The more uncomfortable I felt, the more I swallowed. I don't know what swallows a lot, but I looked like it. I looked like something weird. It was everything making me nervous, the glass floor as people glided across the lobby, the chandelier that hung from the center of the roof. So many people, everywhere, talking, laughing, dressed in clothes that were surely worth far more than my ticket to Brisbane. The dresses that filled the room were the kind of dresses Daisy and I used to steal. We used to sell them to survive.

We entered another grand room. I think that's how you would describe it. Grand as in big, like a ballroom you see in old movies... not that I had seen many old movies, but it was how people described them. Heavy hung velvet curtains, waiters carrying glasses filled with champagne, women in colours and men in suits, it was grand, so very grand. I had never seen anything like it before and I began to choke, like the air had been swept out of me by all the beauty and grace that surrounded me. I choked out to DB, 'I don't think I should b...' but before I could finish my sentence he grabbed my hand and said, 'we'll get a drink.' Then he swept me across the room like the ugly duckling that turned into a swan. I felt like that swan as DB held my hand. Deep within I knew that I was still an ugly duckling, but it was something about him, the way he made me feel when he smiled at me, the way he made me feel when he held my hand, when he comforted me, I didn't feel like that old duck no more.

When we reached the bar I picked up the first glass I could see and I skulled that drink in one go. The fizz almost burnt out my nostrils and my eyes went all watery. Still I grabbed another glass as quick as I could and took another large gulp, staring everyone down as I did. Wondering if they could see through this swans facade?

'David Burgess!' came this high-pitched voice that really was over the top.

I turned around to see this fat faced, busy bee, squeezed into a dress that was two sizes too small and I hoped it wasn't his mother. Oh God I hoped his parents weren't there. The thought had not crossed my mind earlier, but imagine if they saw me! Jesus this isn't good I thought and I took another gulp of champagne, then realised I knew his name! It was Dave!

'David, so nice to see you again. And who is your friend?' she asked.

'This is Lisa,' he said, smiling as he touched my back and I felt like that swan again. Maybe it was the booze making me feel like a swan (I drank those two glasses really quickly), but as soon as I realised he had called me Lisa, the swan feeling disappeared. He didn't know my real name.

The woman held out her hand toward me and said, 'charmed.'

OK I thought, but charmed by her I was not.

'Gladys Ferro. Lisa?'

She was waiting for my last name. Damn it! Here we go again. 'Pennyworth,' I said. That name just hadn't shaken off. I started to rhyme in my mind, 'pick a penny see it luck all night long you…' wait, that's not how it goes (think I was drunk).

'Pennyworth. British? Let me guess, your family comes from a long line of politicians just like our David Burgess here?'

I shook my head in disagreement.

'Public services? Education?' she said in her high-pitched voice, which was really annoying.

'No,' I said. This woman clearly wasn't going to shut up.

'Oh good, I was worried you going to be one of those talkers, you know, teachers and social workers, all they do is talk, talk, talk, talk, never know when to stop, drives you mad.'

Dave rolled his eyes at me and I almost laughed.

'Will you excuse us Mrs. Ferro? Damian is expecting us.'

'Oh of course David.'

As Dave (I hoped I could call him Dave, short for David), waited for someone to clear out of our way, Mrs. Ferro said to me, 'Damian is going to be quite the politician isn't he? It's in our blood, a natural talent. What is in your blood Miss Pennyworth?'

I couldn't help myself, it may have been the booze, the dress, the fact that Dave was leading me away, but I said, 'booze, coke that sort of thing.' I'm not sure if she heard me, if I was too far away, but she certainly had a confused look on her face, which made me laugh. Was that mean? Ah who cares, I was feeling free! Another glass of that white bubbled stuff please!

Dave led me toward... hey I said Dave again! David is his name and don't you forget it! Sorry, I got excited by the fact that I knew his name! Completely forgetting the brutal lie of Lisa Pennyworth. Anyway, Dave led me toward his brother. I really didn't like Damian and now I know why. The first thing out of his mouth was, 'David.' Like Dave was in trouble. Like a parent calls out when you have broken something and put it back in the cupboard, hoping nobody would notice, but they found it!

'No need to be so formal,' Dave responded.

'I've been trying to call you all afternoon. You should not have brought her here.'

Damian looked at me the way I was used to, with disgust... and just like that the ugly duckling was back, the nobody was here, the homeless girl revealed. I felt naked in a room full of people I didn't know.

'It was your idea mate,' Dave told him.

'She's trash, just like I told you.'

'Dame you're out of line!'

'Am I? You should have heard what the little...'

'Enough!' Dave cut him off, 'what is your problem?'

Retracting into myself, I felt more worthless in that moment in that stupid dress than I would have felt in my own clothes, on my own turf, the streets.

'I'm outta here!'

I threw it out of my mouth with hate, with disgust of this arsehole who didn't even know me. Why did Dave even take me there? I threw his hand away and made my way back through the thick crowd as quickly as I could, not looking at anyone, not even breathing, scared that if I blew one breath out that a tear, a gasp of air or a whimper may leave my lips. I don't cry! I haven't felt anything since, I don't even remember anymore. What I did know, is that I didn't want to feel that feeling, not ever again. Why did I go? What was I doing? I questioned myself as I sped across the lobby repeating to myself, 'I'm just a homeless girl, I'm just a homeless girl.'

As I walked outside, I heard Dave call my fake name.

'Lisa, Lisa wait!'

I felt even worse by the simple fact that I had lied about my name.

'I'm going. Just leave it.'

'I'm sorry I…'

I cut him off, 'leave it.'

I didn't want to talk about it, I wanted to run, but run where? Samm was at Brado's maybe? I didn't really know. I was wearing a stupid dress, playing stupid dress ups to be like those stupid girls. I was confused and I wanted to run, but I had nowhere to go.

I started walking and Dave walked with me. I was cold and started to shiver. Dave took off his coat and wrapped it around my shoulders.

'He doesn't know you,' he said.

But isn't that the problem. Nobody knows me but they all treat me that way. Everyone has treated me that way. Except for Dave, which just made me feel suspicious of him. I found myself asking did I miss something here? Am I about to get screwed over by this guy?

When I was a little girl and something bad had happened, like my mother punching the crap out of me, I'd pretend I was in fairyland. I would run outside and dance across the land, waiting to be rescued from the evil witch, but no one came. No one rescued me.

'I don't need you to rescue me.'

I gave Dave back his coat. I was Ange, strong. I'd been through worse before.

We walked for a while in silence. He didn't push me. He didn't ask anything nor expect me to talk. He just let me walk. We came across a cab and Dave opened the door and held it open for me to step inside. When we got back to his place we stood inside for a couple of seconds in silence, which to me felt like another long gift card of awkwardness. I wondered if he felt as awkward as I did. Before the moment could go on any longer I said, 'night' and walked off into that second bedroom, shutting the door behind me. I fell onto the bed and wondered how I got to this point? Why did I go to that stupid ball in the first place? Why did I care what he thought? Why did I care so much? Why did I care about this person? I care about this person? I care about Dave? Oh Christ, I cared about Dave.

CHAPTER THIRTY SEVEN

HE MEANS MORE
TO ME NOW

I woke up the next morning in a bit of a daze. Does he like me? Was the question that was running through my mind. I found myself circling images of what would happen next; a life for Sammy and I with Dave. I pictured it somehow working, with Sammy and Dave becoming the best of mates. I'd forgotten everything that was really going on. It was as though I didn't have a care in the world. It was weird, I'd never done that before, staying in bed for what felt like hours, having no idea of time. I was smiling warm in bed, picturing a life, a real life. I couldn't remember ever doing that. I'd never really let myself imagine the better, because it never came. It would be giving me false hope. But on that particular day I was imagining amazing things and it was making me feel wonderful. Had I ever even used that word before? Wonderful? I don't think so. I don't remember that being part of my vocabulary. Then I got real silly with my imagination. I pictured his mum loving me, becoming like best friends. Ridiculous huh! I imagined us having not much to do with his Dad and Damian apologizing to me. It's when I got to that part I shook my head far from out of the clouds. What a joke, to let myself get carried away like that! Had I forgotten what had happened the night before? I guess so. But now that I had remembered, it was time to face reality. None of it was real and one thing I hated more than being homeless was having false hope and that's all it was, false hope.

I rolled myself out of bed, shoulders a little more rounded by the defeat of the previous night. The reality of how things really were snapped me back into focus. I made my way to the bathroom and could hear Dave typing away on his laptop in the kitchen. I wondered if he had changed his mind, if he had re-written the article. I decided I was going to ask him.

I showered first and found more clothes to wear from one of the bags. I kept my jeans on and my underwear (there wasn't any of those in the bags). I found a T-shirt that kind of fitted; well it didn't look too bad I guess. I took a deep breath in and reminded myself of who I was, Ange that strong homeless girl.

I switched off my emotions as though flicking a light off and walked into the kitchen.

'Hi,' Dave said, looking at me with that dimpled smile.

Focus! I thought to myself.

I responded with a squeaky, 'hi.'

'Did you sleep alright?'

'Yes,' I replied, even though I tossed and turned all night.

'Would you like some toast?'

I nodded yes. My stomach was growling at me again. I normally ignore it, but when you have bread on tap, you have to pay attention to it and feed it.

'I was thinking...' I said as Dave popped the bread in the toaster, 'can I read the article you wrote?'

'Yes, of course I can go one better than that,' he said with the hugest smile on his face.

I couldn't help but smile back as I asked, 'what do you mean?'

He looked outside as the sun poured in through the windows. 'Let's take this outside and I'll show you.'

He buttered the toast thick just as I like it. He even put a piece of cheese on it and I wondered if heaven was something like this? Someone making you hot toast coated in butter and cheese in the morning. It really was my favorite thing.

We sat outside on the couch swing and Dave handed me his laptop. It was much lighter than I expected. The one I used to type on (the one Ty got for me) was heavy and thick. I was afraid to use it at the start. I mean what did I need it for? But Ty said it was good to play games and that I needed to learn. He said the internet would be big and he was right! Google didn't exist back then, well not that I knew of, but I couldn't imagine not being able to Google stuff now. I don't know why, it's not like I had anything to Google about, but Sammy and I would sometimes use the computer in the library. I knew it was important to show him if I was going to get him to go back to school. Samm would Google stuff like killer snakes or the most annoying sound in the world. It was pretty funny stuff. Anyway, I began to read as Dave sat next to me. Page after page it was like I was reading a story. One story. My story. It wasn't exactly in the right order and the details weren't one hundred per-cent correct but it was all the stories I had told him linked together.

'What is this?' I asked him.

'It's all of the stories you told me.'

'But it's as though it's one story?' I was a little confused.

'I couldn't sleep last night with what Dames said and… I thought, why couldn't it be? One story.'

I still wasn't really following.

'What do you mean?' I asked.

'What if it was a book? A way to tell others a complete story? If Damian knew, he wouldn't act like such a jerk. We can fix it up, together? They're your stories… well your stories of other people. You know what I mean.'

His eyes smiled at me like a star that twinkles at night. I understood what he was saying, but all those stories were really all MY stories. They were me. I just made out as though they happened to other girls. I wasn't sure I wanted people to know all of that. What if they found out it was all about me? The way they would look at me, what they would say? The embarrassment would sink in through my skin and turn me inside out. I'm not sure I could handle being so naked to everyone else.

'You don't have to be homeless. This could be your way out.'

He said it to me with such sincerity, I almost believed him. Could it be possible? Could it actually happen? Is it a joke? Or some kind of trick? I looked around me as though I would see someone laughing or jumping out of the bushes with a camera, like the joke was on me, but Dave kept looking straight at me with eyes so sincere. Then I remembered! My name! I had to tell him my real name!

Dave, my name…'

KNOCK KNOCK KNOCK KNOCK came from inside, cutting me off and sounding as though a brick was being hit repeatedly against the front door, stopping me from saying anymore.

Dave got up and went inside to answer the door. As soon as I heard the yelling, I knew who it was. I walked inside and stood in the hallway out of sight, listening to the screaming match that was taking place.

'Jesus Dave! I overheard her telling that black kid that she is going to rip you off. The pair of them are heading north.'

Damian spoke it as though Dave was an idiot... but how the hell did he know that? I hadn't seen him since that first day I came to Dave's house. Had he seen me? Or heard me? Was he there yesterday when I saw Samm? I was confused, asking questions I had no answers to.

'Bullshit!' Dave snapped back.

I really wished to myself that it was bullshit. I didn't know whether to run or to see it out. Fear gripped me to my spot, but it was fear of Dave hating me, not fear of the situation I was in.

'For Christ sake, is there any reason why I would make it up? You're my little brother.'

'Here we go, like you're looking out for me. We should call you Bill Junior!'

'Maybe we should call Bill,' Damian argued back.

'Every time I have a small bit of success, you come along and ruin it. Not this time,' Dave said, assured to stand his ground.

I felt like I was caught up in an old argument of years of resentment. The subject matter was me, but the argument was old.

I moved closer to the door as Damian spat out more words in anger.

'She's a street kid Dave, nothing but a research project, you said it yourself. Use her to wind up the old man. You just couldn't keep your dick in your pants.'

'Enough!' Dave said it with enough push to scare anyone out.

'Do you really think you can take her home? Meet the parents? Swap stories of eating out of bins?'

I'd never eaten out of a bin! What the fuck was he talking about! Now I was angry! At the both of them! Research project? What the hell? Had I been had? Used again? Used as a tool to piss off his dad! I wanted to kick and scream, but for some reason I didn't move, I was frozen. It was like I had something major to lose that I didn't want to let go of.

'You have no idea, but then again why would you? Spoon-fed, favours for candidacy. Who do you think voted you in? You haven't had to work for it. It all comes so easily doesn't it!'

'Last night was work and you and your little street rat causing a scene like that did not help!'

'You're a fraud,' Dave spat back at Damian. 'Who is dad paying off this time? Or is he writing the funding cheque himself?'

'You think you've got what it takes to be a journo?' Damian said with spite. 'That strings weren't pulled for you? You're truly pathetic. Dad can't stand you. You'll go running back home, but he's already cut you off. He knows as well as I do, you'll never get that job at the Journal. You'll end up on the streets with that whore!'

By the look on Damian's face, it was just as much as a surprise to him as it was to me, as Dave punched him across the face. Damian's head fell to the side in one quick motion and as he corrected the fall and looked back up at Dave, he let out another secret, 'so that's the way it is? Well ask your whore where your gold ring is? And while you're at it, ask her, her real name!'

With those words Damian turned and walked away.

Dave slammed the door behind him, then turned around and looked at me with a mix of anger, disappointment and disillusionment.

'Is it true? Are you planning to rip me off?'

I didn't know how to answer his question, so I said nothing.

He then blurted out, 'I just hit my brother in the face for you. Did you steal my ring?'

'No, I...'

'Did you?'

'Yes! But it's not what you think!'

'Isn't it? You should leave.'

He turned his back on me and I turned to leave the room, but something stopped me. I wanted him to know that I wasn't going to go through with it.

'I did steal it. I gave it to Sammy to sell, but yesterday when I saw him, I told him to get it back. I didn't know you. I thought you were using me like everyone else.'

'And that makes it OK? Lisa? Is that even your real name?'

Shit shit shit shit! Repeated in my head. I was just about to tell him my real name before Damian spilt the beans!

'I was just about to tell you...'

'Just go.' He cut me off.

'Dave, listen to me. I had to be careful with who knew my name.'

'Why is that? The police after you too?'

'No, it's Lizzy. What I did for her. I'm in trouble for that. Serious trouble.'

'Why would I believe you?'

'Because I'm telling you the truth!'

'Really? The girl who trusts no one is telling me the truth!'

'My name is Ange!' I pleaded out.

I wanted him to believe me. More than anything I wanted him to believe me.

'It's Angela Browski,' but what was the use in telling him? 'You don't give a shit anyway. You were using me. All I am is a research project. What fix me up? Use my stories? Get rid of me when you got what you wanted? You're just like everyone else. Use me to piss off your dad. That's why you invited me last night? Make me wear that stupid dress!'

'No... yes... you don't understand.'

'Really, I don't understand! To think I actually thought you wanted to help me. I'm just research.'

'You're not... you were research.'

He paused. 'You're not... I want...'

Then the most unexpected thing happened, he pulled me in, all the way in. He put his arms around me and his hand on the back on my neck.

'I want to help you.'

I didn't flinch. I didn't move.

When he released me he told me, 'I wanted to piss him off, my father, but just as much as I wanted to show him you. It was him I was fighting with yesterday morning on the phone. I was trying to get him to do something, I don't even really know what.'

'I'm sorry Dave, I wanted to tell you my real name but I thought it was too late. I didn't want you to hate me.'

'I don't hate you.'

'Even though I took your ring?'

'Can you get it back? My grandma gave it to me.'

I nodded yes, feeling ashamed. I could see how much he loved his gran. I wanted all of my stupid mistakes to go away. I felt embarrassed and wanted him to say something else, change the subject so I could get rid of the yucky feeling that was crawling all over my skin.

As though knowing the regret was taking me over, with the signs of red embarrassment welling up in my face, Dave gently touched my cheek and said, 'I'm going after Damian OK.'

'OK.'

'OK.'

Then he walked out the door.

CHAPTER THIRTY EIGHT

···

SO I'M
ANGELA BROWSKI

So I'm Angela Browski. There was no more hiding... except he still didn't know that all the stories I told him were actually mine, as in all the stories were me, about me. I decided that fact did not need to be told. I could leave it the way it was.

It was sort of weird after what happened with Damian. When Dave held me, I never wanted it to end, but it did end. I wondered if he felt sorry for me or if I was worth more to his writing career then booting me out the door?

When Dave got back after looking for Damian he told me he couldn't find him, that he would try and call him again tomorrow. He suggested we work through the book and I agreed. I was going to help him write it. It was worth doing, right? It was still a chance to change our lives and if nothing changed, then I guess it gave me a little more time with Dave. If I continued to help write the whole book, that would mean we'd have to stay in Sydney a little longer. I decided to wait until the next day to tell Sammy. I found myself asking if we were going to leave at all? I guess that was something I had to decide.

I felt torn. Not really sure of what was happening, but knowing that the book could be our one and only chance to get off the streets for good; a real way, a lasting way, a legit way. I'd forgotten about Pho and Jase. I felt safe at Dave's place. I guess I was still lying to him, wasn't I? He didn't know the real reason why I left Melbourne. If I told him, then the dream would be over and I couldn't do that. There was no way he would understand.

Later that night, Dave and I were sitting at the kitchen table, munching on corn chips (they were really good). I wasn't really prying, but I wanted to know why his dad was so anti Dave. I mean, I know why he would be anti me, most people are, but Dave was kind and passionate... he was really super smart.

'I was editor of my university paper. It's a big thing for someone studying political science. I finished my degree with honours, more to keep my father happy then because I wanted to. I thought it would soften the blow when I suggested a change to journalism.'

Dave sighed like it was hopeless, like it was the silly dream of a five-year-old wanting to fly to space.

'My father almost disowned me. He threatened to kick me out and spread the word to ruin a career that had not yet started. Pretty extreme huh?'

I nodded, but I didn't think it was extreme. I mean, look at my past... dads suck.

'I chose to do my masters in international relations,' he continued, 'figuring it would keep him happy and off my back while I kept writing in the background.'

'Will you finish your masters?' I asked. Not really sure of what a masters was, but I didn't want to look stupid either. I figured Dave was way smarter than me with all that education. I don't know how he sat in a classroom for so long, for six extra years! Made me feel suffocated by the restriction of it all.

'I can finish the last two subjects via correspondence. It wouldn't be a complete waste. The job is with the Journal, a political and financial magazine, so it is a perfect fit. I thought he would be happy with that. I wanted to leave Canberra on good terms, show him what a great opportunity it was, but instead he basically told me not to come back.'

'It's not so bad. You've still got this place, even if you have to fold pamphlets for a douche.'

'Dame isn't a bad person. I have not hit him like that since I was twelve when he stole my girlfriend. Hmmm, it was not the only time he did that. Good looks and charm have always oozed out of him. I simply cannot understand why he is always in competition with me. Sometimes it clouds his judgment. When we were kids, we were really close, but something happened, our family changed. I hit my head pretty bad one year, was in hospital for weeks. The first few hours were critical, I needed a lot of blood from my father. The whole situation changed him. It was almost as if he couldn't handle losing me. Maybe he couldn't handle losing any of us. Anyway, after that he pushed us all away, mum started drinking heavily and now they barely speak to each other.'

Dave looked up at the ceiling as though searching for an answer that had never come to him.

'Maybe it runs in the family. I did not know my grandfather very well, but apparently he was really hard on my father. He died a long time ago when I was five. The only thing I remember from his funeral was Gran never cried. Gran was sweet and good to Dame and I. She was always helping out at church... it always made me wonder how bad my grandfather must have been that she did not shed one tear for him.'

'People are shit,' I said. Not exactly comforting but Dave shrugged his shoulders and smiled.

'I tried to get my father to care after all those stories you told me, but he said the Journal was turning me into a raving loony, that I was wasting his time. I know there are rules and procedures and limitations to what he can do, but I thought I had a direct link to Parliament, that maybe he would help in some way or at least direct me to the right people. It's like he can't hear me anymore. I've pissed him off so badly, he's flicked a switch. I wanted him to care.'

'Some people don't want to care,' I told him.

'Hmmm… maybe we can change that.'

I snorted a laugh and said 'OK, if you can get them to care, I'll give you a medal.'

That made Dave smile.

'You know that dress wasn't stupid,' he said still smiling.

I went bright red.

I didn't know what to say as he kept smiling at me. I grabbed a handful of corn chips and shoved them in my mouth, later kicking myself for looking like a pig! What was I thinking! Shoving a fist full in. Dave then said goodnight and went to bed. He said he was exhausted from the previous sleepless night. God I hope it wasn't the corn chips!

I decided to stay up and read over Dave's words, what he had written on the laptop, what he had pieced together. As my eyes darted across the screen, absorbing all the written words, some kind of energy was alert within me, pricked up, ready. It was like my hands became part of the keys on the board, moving as fast as the thoughts came in and out of my brain. They were rushing through my mind, not stopping, not thinking, just typing. Flash after flash I saw the pictures. I was writing my story. Raw real pieces. The out of order stories I put back into the original flow, exactly how they happened to me. I didn't stop to think of what I would tell Dave, how I would say it, or what I would do to explain the differences. Would

I tell him that this was actually me? Could I? All I could see in that moment were images of my years on the streets becoming words on a page. My whole life was vibrating, pulsating, flying out of me; being told. This was me, Angela Browski, telling it like it is.

In the morning I woke up to a tapping noise on the kitchen window. I squinted my eyes open and looked at the laptop. I'd fallen asleep at the table, head down, half across the keyboard. There was another round of tapping which caught my attention. I looked up at the window, blinking myself awake and focused in on Sammy's face.

'Ange,' he muffled through the glass.

I got up and went toward the back door, but he waved no at me and mouthed, 'the park' and pointed toward the back of the house. I understood what he meant. There was a park down the end of the road. I would meet him there. I made sure the laptop had saved the changes I made and closed the lid quietly. I tiptoed past Dave's bedroom and walked out the front door, taking minutes to close it gently, silently, as to not wake him up

As I reached the park Samm grabbed me and pushed me against a tree. He was trying to hide me... hide us.

'Ya in trouble A.'

I never heard worry in Samm's voice, not worry for our lives ever, but those words were chilling like

I already knew the sentence that was about to come next.

'What are you talking about? I've got news Sammy, good news.'

I said it with a smile... hell! I said it with gleaming beams shooting out the corners of my turned upward lips! We had a fairytale ending unfolding in front of us. This book was going to get us out of trouble. I knew it would.

'Listen A!' he yelled at me. 'Pho is here!'

Has your head ever gone blank? Like really blank? Like a cloud swiped away your face, taking with it all of your memories and any future that you might have had? This was how I felt in that moment. My heart, my being, it sank into the ground. It dropped so fast, I could have vomited right there in that moment, if only I could have moved. Without realising, I had in fact moved inches away from the tree. Sammy grabbed me, forcing me back against its trunk, shielding me from the view of the road.

'He was here last night and he got people Ange, they're looking for ya. They know ya here. He wanna kill you!'

I heard the words but my brain was darting around inside itself, searching for an answer that did not exist. My legs went to jelly and I felt myself sliding down the tree. I was giving up. I was letting go. Why had I fought so hard, when all I do is end up right back here?

Sammy snapped me into attention, pulling me up onto my feet.

'Jase is with em. Jase got people too. Ya gotta get outta here.'

He started to shake me but it was as though I was standing outside of my body, not fully comprehending the blow that had hit me. I was unable to respond.

'Ange! Ange are ya listening?! We gotta leave!'

Sammy held me close and looked straight into my eyes, 'grab as much money as you can. I'll do the same. Go!'

He pushed me in the direction of Dave's house, but how did he know? 'How do you know?' I asked him.

'All the bro's know. They don't know that I know you.'

He paused and I knew something bad was coming.

'A, they got Ty, real bad.'

Real bad? Real bad? What does that mean? Real bad? I didn't ask, I couldn't ask. It was as though I already knew the answer. He saved my life and this whole week in Sydney, I hadn't given him much more than a thought at all. He was still protecting me, still giving his life for me and I am here, believing in some stupid dream. Some fairytale, like I could possibly be a real life Cinder-fucking-rella. I hated myself for that. A deep-seated hate.

I broke down, I sobbed. Why God? Fuck you! These are good people and you kill them in such hate!

Why do you do this why!!!!!!!!!!!!!

I screamed so loud from within my heart, I was sure every fiber, every piece of tissue encased in my chest exploded. It flew about my body spilling hatred everywhere. Hatred of God, hatred of my life, hatred of all the people I had lost because of me! It was all my fault.

Samm grabbed my face. 'Ya can't do nothing but run. Ya hear me? Meet me at the laneway, we'll get the train out.'

He pushed me away and I ran. I ran back to Dave's place, not knowing, not thinking, unable to see what was in front of me, let alone comprehend what had just happened, what it all meant?

I ran through the front door of Dave's house not blinking, not even seeing if he was there. I just ran. Jumper, money, what do I need? I was making an imaginary list of stuff that I didn't even have.

'What am I doing!' I screamed at myself, confused, not knowing what to do.

I found myself in the bedroom searching for... I wasn't sure. My jumper that's right, I needed my jumper.

'What are you doing?' Dave asked from behind.

I couldn't face him. I couldn't look at him. I began to sob. Where would I even start?

'Ange? What's wrong?'

I could hear the concern in his voice, as I felt his arms turn me around, melting me into his care.

'He's gonna kill me, he's gonna kill me,' I sobbed through breaths.

He lifted my face from off his chest.

'Who is going to kill you? What are you talking about?'

He sat me on the bed and knelt down in front of me. His big eyes filled with so much concern and there I was about to break his heart, his trust of me and his care of me with the brutal reality of my past.

'That's why I came here. Ty put me and Sammy on a bus. It's my fault. I got jumped. I was setup. I didn't want to tell you, I didn't want you to think of me as just some.. ' I choked on my words, 'I was delivering and I got jumped.'

There I said it! And now he would hate me forever.

'The stories, that's you? That's your Ty?'

He looked away ashamed of me. He rubbed his face wishing it would all go away, that I would go away.

'I had to do it. It was the only way. Dave? Dave look at me?' I pleaded.

He looked at me, but didn't know what to say, so he turned his head and I could feel pieces of me shattering to the floor.

'I have to leave. Pho will kill me. Ty saved my life for no reason, cause now we're both dead!'

I stood to leave, to take my bad luck and my pain far away from him, but he grabbed my arm, urging me to stay.

'I, I just…'

'I don't have time,' I screamed. 'Don't you understand? He is going to kill me!'

'There must be a way?'

'There's not, there's nothing, there's…' I shouted in his face, 'if I don't find twenty-five grand, I'm dead!'

I sobbed in his arms. I sobbed for the fear of death that finally came knocking on my door. TAKE ME! I screamed from the core of my bones wanting to split every single one of them and for each tiny piece to shard me, cut me up from the inside out. TAKE ME DEATH! I cried out, you've been knocking on my door my whole damn life! Why do you leave me still alive??

Dave held my head and let me cry.

'We can find a way,' he finally said.

'But how?' I asked.

How could he possibly find that much money?

'I need to make a phone call,' was all that he said.

I was too drained to find a way of understanding his words. I nodded and followed him to the front room. I curled myself up on the couch and dazed at the TV. There was a lot of stuff on the telly about Dave's dad and the government. Dave told me his dad was the Australian Treasurer, but I had no idea what that meant. Something important I guess, as his father's face flashed across the screen a lot. Something big was going on, something political, but I didn't even know what political meant, not really. I could not compute it and I did not care. My brain hurt, my eyes felt like strings that had been played way too hard, strained, shooting pain into the back of my head. I sat comatosed as Dave walked into the other room talking to someone on the other end of his phone. I had to meet Samm soon and tell him of the plan, our plan... Dave's plan.

I think my eyes may have closed. It felt like I lost hours but no time had passed by. I really had no idea if it had been five minutes or five hours. Dave walked back into the room and said good-bye to the person on the other end of the phone. Instead of looking at me, giving me any clue of what or who it was that he was talking to, he looked straight at the TV as it announced, 'the government has been dissolved.'

'Shit,' came out of Dave's mouth and his phone began to ring again. He answered it, 'oh, ah, hi mum,' then he walked back into the kitchen.

I had no idea what that meant, dissolved? Maybe it was like the Wicked Witch of the West, when Dorothy threw water over her, dissolving her onto the ground. Perhaps they did something wrong? Whatever it was, it wasn't good, I could tell by Dave's face and the protestors screaming on the telly.

My head was pounding, so I searched for the remote, which was lying on the floor. I turned off the TV, ending the screeches and noticed a magazine poking out from underneath the couch. It was the

Journal. The magazine Dave was writing for. It sat open on the page of the article Dave wrote about me.

'Drain on taxpayer dollars. This girl has no remorse and a clear acceptance of stealing from hard working Australians. This particular street kid has no intention of using any resources to educate or gain employment. Every year, as taxes rise, so do costs allocated to social workers, public housing and wasted resources within the public sector.'

It got worse. It went on and on about how bad I was, about what a waste of space I was. I had been had again! He didn't write anything of what I told him. Not one single story. Perhaps he was doing the same with the book? It was all a lie to get my stories and turn them all against me! Show the world what a whore I was and all the bad things that I had done. The joke was on me!

As I continued to read the words I could hear him on the phone to his mother in the other room.

'I can't talk about her right now. It's complicated… Mum leave it, it's nothing.'

Nothing! I'm nothing! Ty is dead! I am still here and I am nothing! After all that bullshit he told me yesterday, the sob story about his dad, how he touched my face, twinkled his eye and convinced me he wanted to help by writing this damn book! I had to run. I was running away again.

I ran straight into that spare room and slammed the door shut. I circled the room, searching again for what I needed. It was time for me to go.

'What are you doing?' Dave asked, bursting through the door.

'I'm going,' I said and threw the magazine at him.

'It's not what you think. Well it is, but it was before we started writing together.'

'You said you changed it!'

'I did, I sent the new one two days ago. I don't know what happened.'

Why would I believe him? It was all lies. My lies, his lies, lies!

'I knew this was a mistake,' I said, as Dave grabbed me by the arm.

'What's a mistake?'

I took his hand off me and threw it away.

'Well go on! Why don't you tell your precious mother about me?' I began to mimic him like a schoolgirl, 'no one, it's complicated, it's nothing. What's the matter Dave? Can't tell your mum about the homeless girl you live with?'

'Come on it's not like that. She wouldn't under…'

'Stand,' I said, cutting him off. 'Right, she wouldn't understand.'

'Look Ange, with everything that is going on, it's a little hard to tell my mother. You have to understand this is not normal for me and certainly not for my parents.'

'That's right, I'm not normal and I'll never be normal. I'll always be that girl who lived on the streets.'

'You know that's not true.'

'Oh no -A drain on society, chooses to steal, uneducated...' I said mocking him again, repeating what I had read in the article. 'Should I go on?'

'It was before I knew you.'

'Really? So you didn't use me? God forbid I ever did meet your family. I'd have to lie about my past, so you and your rich parents could feel comfortable in your make believe world. Act like some rich snob, like your mum.'

'You don't know my mother or my family!' he shouted in a pissed off tone.

'I know enough to never want to know her. Someone who hangs out at tennis clubs, sipping chardonnay, marrying rich men for social points. It's disgusting.'

'You have no right commenting on what you know nothing about. My parents worked hard...'

'And I guess, I didn't work hard enough, is that right?'

'Well maybe if you...'

'What?'

'Helped yourself for Christ sake!'

'I did everything I could!'

'You didn't use the services available to you!'

'There was nothing available to me!' I yelled back at him.

We were shouting over the top of each other, both full of anger, hurting each other deliberately to even out the last blow, the last hateful comment.

'Well obviously, you didn't try hard enough to…'

'Try hard enough?'

'You don't just accept that's it, that's the way life is, you work, you push yourself!'

Was this guy fucking joking? Did he not read all the stories, did he not piece two and two together and see it was my whole life? How was that suppose to work out differently? How the fuck was I suppose to change that? It crushed my soul that someone would think I wanted this! Everyday I tried and everyday I suffered. Nothing helped me. No one wanted to help me. Ty, Daisy, Lucy for a day and Sammy. That's it, that's all I had! What the fuck do you want from me!

'What could I do?' I growled at him. 'All I knew was to steal, sell drugs… should I have sold my body too?'

The shouting got louder.

'Ange don't…'

'Should I have done that?'

'That's not what…'

Yes Dave you asked for it! Here it comes! The cold light of fucking day! The reality, the sad truth of my shit existence. Here you go Dave, can you handle it now!

'Fuck a few men?' I shouted.

'I don't want to hear about you whoring yourself!'

He said it. He yelled it. Exactly what he thinks. Exactly what they all think. What they all see me as. What my mother saw me as. It's what she used to call me ever since I could remember and I hadn't even seen her since I was twelve.

'You have no idea what it's like to stay awake all night fearing for your life, starving, knowing it's too late.' I said it with grief, with sadness, with defeat.

Then it happened. My worst fear. My worst moment. It came out. I told him, 'I was sixteen when I was held down, injected with heroin… yeah that story was really about me too!'

It was the Jase story.

'It's not true, it's not…' Dave pleaded through a quivered voice.

I grabbed his face in my hands, 'it's true! That's how Ty found me. He rescued me. Did you want to know that!'

He pulled away from me but I continued, 'would you tell your Mum that? Would you Dave?' I pulled at his T-shirt as he turned away from me again. I kept going, rage built so far up spilling out of me and onto him. 'Would you tell her that old men slept with me? That I am a dirty little whore?'

He pulled further away from me, gripping the windowsill with his hands.

'That maybe you're one of those men? That I'm whoring myself to you? Is that what she would think? Would she?'

'Enough! Enough!' Dave howled, as he shoved his fist through the plastered bedroom wall. 'God, I can't take it anymore. I can't change your past, I can't... it's too much!'

'Damian was right... I don't belong here!'

I turned and walked toward the door, then turned around and looked at him once more.

'A whore could never love you,' I paused, 'WELL I'M NOT A WHORE!' I screamed it and ran out of the house, slamming the front door.

The bright sun blinded me, as my head was swimming with rage, grief, love, loss, confusion. I stopped and composed myself before beginning to walk down the footpath again. I wiped my face and told myself to suck it up. I needed to get clear.

'Ange! Angela!'

I heard my name being called out and turned around to see Damian's red convertible. I immediately turned my head in the opposite direction and kept walking straight, not giving him a second thought.

He drove his car up onto the gutter, pulled the handbrake up and jumped over the door.

'Hey! Look, I know you don't like me but wait!'

I stopped and turned to him.

'Why?' I asked. 'I'm trash remember? Why would you wanna come near me?'

I fastened my pace but he jumped in front of me blocking my path.

'I was just looking out for my brother.'

I stopped just to show him that I knew that comment was full of shit. I didn't know the guy and he didn't know me, but one thing I did know is that he didn't care about me.

'OK, so we don't like each other,' he said with a slimy smile.

'What do you want?' I asked.

'I have something beneficial for the both of us.'

I almost snorted, rolled my eyes and kept walking.

'OK wait, look, I screwed up. Pretty big actually and now there is going to be an early election. The 25k, I'll put it up. I'll publicize your book as my idea. You get the money now, I appeal to the public, help Dave out,' he paused, '... and possible minister for housing I guess.' He said that last bit with distaste.

I had no idea what he meant about minister or election. I may have folded those pamphlets but I didn't read them and as for him as a person, all I knew was how he treated me and Dave. Would he really give me twenty-five grand?

I looked at him knowing that he had the deal of a lifetime for me. It was my ticket out, but Dave hated me now. Could I do the deal anyway? If I did, Samm and I would be free. We'd never have to look over our shoulders, never having to worry about the day Pho caught up with us, which he would. I knew this was our only chance. I had to take it.

I looked back at Dave's house and then at Damian.

'Are you ok?' he asked me.

'Like you care. You really have the money?'

'I was on my way to tell D man.'

I knew it wasn't safe for me to be on the streets of KX, but Samm was down there. I had to rescue him. We said we would meet at Brougham Lane, so that was where I was going. I could then get word to Pho that I had his money.

'Can you drop me off at the Cross, then come back and tell Dave?'

'Public service number one.' He winked it at me without physically winking at all, but it was the same action of winking, but done through his smug smile. I hate winking.

We said nothing in the car. We weren't friends. There was nothing further for us to say. We had a business arrangement and that was it. He pulled over by Brougham Lane, where I was meeting Sammy. As I got out of the car I began to say, 'Dave and I, well...' then decided it wasn't a good idea to tell the jerk what had just happened.

'What?' he asked.

'Nothing. Nothing,' I replied.

I closed the door and Damian looked over at a homeless dude asleep near the gutter and said, 'you know it's funny, I never really noticed them before, but I've been seeing them all day.'

And with that he drove away. Yeah funny I thought to myself. Actually it wasn't funny at all. It was shit! All he would ever see me as, is that homeless girl.

I moved up the laneway toward where I thought Samm would be. Once I got to the corner at Vic Street I froze! Just like that day in Melbourne, which felt like a lifetime ago, but was really only seven days ago. Pho was standing across the road. SUDDENLY someone grabbed me from behind and I squealed!

'Shh, shh, Ange it's me.'

'Jesus Christ!' I said to Sammy as we moved away from the edge of the corner.

I hugged him so tight, like it was the first time I had seen him in a year.

'Ya gotta leave Angie. Ya gotta go now!'

'I have the money to pay him.'

'Don't be stupid. Get outta here.'

'But he'll have to take the money.'

'Forget it Ange, he gonna kill ya anyway.'

'There's gotta be a way. I have to go back... you're coming with me.'

'No, someone gotta throw em off. He's got everyone lookin for ya, round the Cross, at the station, everywhere.'

'It's too dangerous,' I said with so much concern. I didn't want us to separate.

'Sometimes ya gotta play the cards that are dealt to ya. I'll take care of me, let me take care of you. I'm not going to lose you too.' Samm said it with such

love, with such care. We looked at each other with the
love of a brother and a sister. It was his turn to look
after me. I was afraid in that moment that I would
never see him again. I wasn't afraid to lose him, I was
afraid of what would happen to him if I was gone. But
he was right, if Pho got me now he would kill me, no
questions asked. I nodded at him in agreement.

'Go straight back to Brado's and wait it out there.
Stay off the streets till you hear from me.' It was my
last commanding instruction of him.

'Okay, just go –Go!' he said, pushing me away.

I gave him a kiss on the cheek and turned, running
down the laneway.

Samm called out, 'A!'

I stopped and turned around as he threw something at me. I caught it and opened up my hand. The
sparkle of reflecting sunlight caught my eye before I
realised it was Dave's gold ring. Thank you Sammy,
I told him with my eyes and continued to run down
the laneway.

I took all the back streets I could possibly find,
constantly looking over my shoulder. I wasn't sure
how I was going to cross the main road back to Dave's
house. I had to weave the streets like it was a maze,
but I could not avoid the dragon's path, the main road.
It was the only way over to Dave's side. I would have
to cross it. I decided to take a street further down the
hill.

As I came toward the bottom of the hill, I stopped and threw myself to the ground, for up ahead was Johnny! I couldn't believe he was there! Tig too I bet. They were the reason I was in this mess to begin with. They certainly would want me dead. I found myself asking questions of why they did that to me? Why did they set me up? But it was pointless. This was a game I was not going to win. So I rolled across the ground and in-between some cars, while wishing I could rip Johnny's throat out. Physically it was impossible with my bare hands, but in that moment I surely wanted to try.

I stayed in-between those two cars, not daring to move for at least five minutes. I checked the road was clear from every angle before bolting further down the hill. The park was up ahead and would give me access to the other side of Vic Street. It was by far my best option... my only option. I sprinted to the bus shelter ten meters away, stopping to ensure I was alone. I peered through the cracks of the shelter's wall and convulsed in fear as I saw Jase! God please! I plead-ed, then stopped myself and decided to plead with Death instead. Death please, you are the one who has been by my side though all of my life. Death you are the one I narrowly escape each time. Please help me through this? Get me out of here! Then a glimmer of reflected light drew my attention toward the water, to the spot where I first talked to Dave, Woolloomooloo Wharf. It was there I could hide out. I closed my eyes and ran. I ran so hard I'm not sure I breathed. I didn't stop. I didn't look, I just ran. I had to make it to the water. So many exits, so many escape routes. I could circle my way back around.

My heart was jumping out of my chest. I was trying to catch it with every breath. As I reached the water I bent down in pain, trying to get a hold of my lungs, trying to stop them from collapsing, from contracting. It was then I felt a pair of arms wrap around me. I struggled to get free.

'NOOOOOO!' I screamed!

'Ange it's me, it's me!'

I turned around, 'Dave?' My newly regrown heart sank back into its rightful spot, in that cave within my chest. It was repaired by just one look at him.

'I thought, I thought something, that they might have, or seen you,' Dave stumbled out. 'I'm sorry. I'm so sorry. Ange, I should never have said anything. I don't care about your past. None of it matters, none of it.' He said it with such honesty, with such sincerity. I believed him. I didn't care what had happened, about the fight we had. I was scared and I needed him.

'They're looking for me.'

'We have the money. Everything is going to be OK.'

'You came for me.'

He held my face in his hands and kissed me, deeply, passionately. The world stopped. Time stood still. I could feel no breeze. I could hear no cars. I could only see the blue of his eyes and feel the soft touch of his lips as they pressed onto mine. My whole being danced as though it was sparked by a beautiful song. I was light. It was as though air did not exist. I felt every inch of his love for me and I felt every inch of how much I loved him.

When our lips parted and reality came back into focus, I told him, 'we've gotta go get Samm.' He nodded at me and pulled me by the hand. He led me to Damian's car, a favour he had asked of him, so that he could find me. When we jumped inside the red convertible that screamed, I AM HERE, I slumped right down to the floor, staying way out of sight.

There were cars everywhere on Victoria Street. I pointed out Brado's, but Dave couldn't park the car, there were no spots. I looked at Dave and nodded that I would be all right, then I jumped over the door and out of the car and straight up the stairs of Brado's hostel. As I pushed my way through the front double doors, the sunlight blinded my eyes. As the sunlit haze cleared, I came face to face with Pho, at the other end of his gun.

'You never run,' were his only words.

He then grabbed me by the throat and choked me up against the wall, letting off one round of bullets just centimeters from my head. This was him showing his power. Scaring me, showing me that I was dead and that the moment he decided it was all over for me would still come as a surprise. He was going to torment me.

'I have your money. I can give you your mon...' but he tightened his grip and cut off my words, strangling me by my neck. I began to lose the battle, letting go of my entire life, feeling as though I was about to pass out through the lack of oxygen that flowed.

In that moment a figure burst through the door and Pho loosened his grip, turning his weapon on DAVE! NO DAVE! GO! I yelled from within.

I had no time to think, Pho would kill him in a second (that much I knew). From deep within me, out came Ty, as he had shown me a thousand times how to get out of that grip. I blocked Pho's arm, I flipped my other arm around, twisting his gun hand as a round went off. I kicked his calf then his heal and pushed him to the ground and held him there by my left arm. His other hand still holding onto the gun was twisted up into his stomach. I didn't wait for his shock to lift or for that moment of realisation of what was about to happen to kick in. I immediately squeezed his finger, which was still on the trigger. I squeezed it twice and let two bullets fill his body.

The shock of the moment sent me flying back against the wall Had I really just shot Pho? It all happened so fast, as though if you didn't live it, you couldn't possibly have seen it. It came quicker than any blow. No time to think, but only to act.

A cough from my right snapped me out of my daze and I turned to look at Dave.

'DAVE! DAVE NO!' I screamed.

I leaped up onto my feet and rushed to his side. He had caught the first round that Pho had let off. I pulled him up into my arms and begged, 'Dave No! Please Dave! I'm sorry!' I sobbed, 'I'm so sorry.' His blood covered my hands and I screamed out, 'HELP, SOMEBODY PLEASE HELP ME!'

Police cars came, ambulance too, but Dave died in my arms that very day.

CHAPTER THIRTY NINE

SURVIVED

I was arrested and kept inside for three weeks while they decided what to do with me. There was no evidence of any criminal activity between Pho and I. Because of my record in Melbourne, it appeared that it was a retaliation attack on Ty. They let me go, agreeing that it was self-defense that killed Pho, who murdered David Burgess.

Samm was in hospital for a couple of weeks. Jase and Tig had beaten him up pretty bad after I left him in Brougham Lane. By the time I got out of prison he had turned sixteen and could do whatever he wanted to do and that was live with me.

Damian honoured our agreement. After the whole Government was dissolved (basically the whole lot of them got the sack), he ran for the seat of Sydney and won. We weren't friends and I think he blamed himself for Dave's death as much as he blamed me. I'm not sure how he could possibly blame himself, we all clearly know it was all me. I think Damian helped me out of memory and respect for Dave, then actually doing it for me.

I had found love. I had found the "one" that everybody talks about, what movies are made about. I found it in just seven days. But my curse, Death, he didn't want anyone to live with me. He wanted me to work alone. For everyone that came close to me died. For some reason Death let Sammy live and Sammy is still by my side. We rebuilt our lives.

I decided if God was to abandon me and Death was to sit at my door, then I was going to do something to stop other girls from having to live a life like this. I was going to take Death far from the streets, far from the girls who cried out every night for somewhere safe to sleep. I was going to make the change. I was going to give them something better than all of this.

Fear stopped me from living. I had feared my whole entire life. I never really lived until I met Dave. I felt more alive in that one week than I had in my entire life. I stopped running and began to live. I started to let go.

It took one person to believe in me and he changed my life forever. Now, much time has passed (a surprise to me, as much as it will be to you), Damian has come back into my life... but that is a story for another time.

Through my eyes, Ange: the life of a street kid.

MORE ON AUTHOR

www.RebeccaDorothy.com

Watch ANGE come to life in the movie 7DAYS

www.uplproductions.com

7DAYS
MOVIE

This Action Crime Drama, spreads from the steps of Parliament House to the Vietnamese gangs of Melbourne, forged with the streets of Kings Cross. This seven-day snapshot will show you unknown worlds, crossing ordinary life with a battle of the streets. A powerful exploration with a political cross, leaves the question of who is really in charge? The fight to hold power means nothing to those on the streets.

David Burgess, the son of the Australian Treasurer, escapes life in Canberra to pursue a career in journalism. Little does he know he is being used as a pawn in a personal vendetta between the Treasurer, the Journal's Editor John Walters and his brother Damian. Dave gets more than he bargained for when his path crosses Ange, a disturbed homeless girl on the run from a drug deal gone wrong. Before long, Dave is caught up in the world of drugs, violence and street gangs.

For one this story ends tragically, sparking a deep desire to fight for justice, for basic human rights.